WILDFLOWER GARDENING

■ Step by Step to Growing Success ■

Yvonne Rees

CROWOOD GARDENING GUIDES

First published in 1991 by
The Crowood Press Ltd
Gipsy Lane, Swindon
Wiltshire SN2 6DQ

British Library Cataloguing in Publication Data

Rees, Yvonne
   Wildflower Gardening.
   1. Great Britain. Gardens. Wild flowering plants.
   Cultivation
   635.967609411

ISBN 1 85223 524 1

Acknowledgements
Special thanks are due to Jackie Elliot, wildflower consultant of Chase Ley, Coggers Lane, Hathersage, Sheffield; to Sally Wood for her help and efficiency with the photographs; to Suzanne for her work on the plant list; and to my husband, family and friends for their help and support.

Picture Credits
All photographs courtesy of the Garden Picture Library:

Clive Boursnell, Fig 55; Brian Carter, Figs 21, 22, 38, 48, 67, 82, 85, 111, 115, 116, 119, 122, 126, 128, 130, 133, 134; Dennis Davis, Figs 24, 36; Robert Estall, Figs 26, 106; Vaughan Fleming, Figs 30, 60, 114, 120, 124; John Glover, Figs 3, 19, 78; Carole Hellman, Fig 108; Marikje Heuff, Figs 14, 28, 41, 46, 49, 117, 118, 135; Roger Hyam, Figs 5, 32, 40, 68, 75, 99, 131; Ann Kelley, Fig 16; Jerry Pavia, Fig 72; Joanne Pavia, Figs 52, 129; Morley-Read, Fig 87; Gary Rogers, Fig 91; David Russell, Figs 35, 51, 56, 58, 62, 64, 88, 123, 127; J.S. Sira, Figs 9, 70, 80, 107, 121; Brigitte Thomas, Figs 1, 7, 11, 12, 76, 112, 125, 132; Didier Willery, Fig 10.

Front cover photograph: John Glover
Back cover photographs: top, Brigitte Thomas; bottom, Robert Estall.

Typeset by Avonset, Midsomer Norton, Bath
Printed and bound by Times Publishing Group Singapore

Contents

Introduction

Like so many others, I first became interested in wild flowers on long walks encompassing a wide range of habitats from marsh and mountain to meadow and hedgerow. Stopping to observe and identify was not just an excuse to slow down and rest; the range of plants and the way they had adapted to cope with their particular environment was fascinating and I loved the natural progression of flowering through the seasons which marked the turning of the year, from the first spring snowdrops to autumn's rich berries and blazing heathers.

I became keen to adapt what I had seen to features back home in my own garden; the impression of a natural brook or stream using boulders bordered by ferns and traditional water's edge plants; a rocky bank displaying some of the more delicate alpines; or a shady area planted with some of my favourite woodland species. It was a natural progression from my interest in herbs and cottage garden plants and I soon noticed an increasing number of wildflower plants and seeds on the lists of the leading herb and specialist nurseries and suppliers.

Over the last few years there has been a huge surge of interest in re-creating wildflower features in our own back gardens. The major flower shows and exhibitions such as Chelsea include at least one wildflower landscape design; children are being encouraged to experiment with natural wildflower habitats as part of their studies; even the town and highway planners are ordering thousands of wild plants to clothe and stabilize the banks and verges.

A wide range of plants is now available, and a wealth of advice and experience has been built up on the best way to propagate and maintain wild plants and how they can be used successfully in a more urban setting. A wild garden provides a lot of pleasure; but there is a more serious benefit to consider, too: that of the plant and animal species we are helping to conserve. Hopefully the ideas and information in this book will inspire you to consider a few wild ideas for your own private patch.

Yvonne Rees
August 1990

Fig 1 (Opposite) *The beautiful tapestry of meadow wild flowers in long grass can be reproduced in quite a small area and provides a great deal of pleasure in return for very little maintenance.*

CHAPTER 1

Why a Wildflower Garden?

Why would anyone choose to have a wildflower garden? Wildflower plants are less predictable to grow than the highly polished hybrids we order from the pages of the glossy seed catalogues. Although some are beautiful in the delicateness of their flowers or real eye-catchers with dramatic foliage, few can match the brilliance of colour or the showiness of double blooms, frills and outsize flowers of so many of the modern varieties. Wild flowers are designed to attract insects with their simple bells, hoods and pompon heads, and maybe a bewitching sweet scent – not humans. Their arresting visual impact is often reliant on the massed effect of their soft colours or shapes, and frequently they will be softened further by the green of long grass or being nestled in a woodland bed of dead bark and leaves. And a wild garden should be large and rambling, at least half an acre in size and quite beyond the scope of the town or city gardener. Also, being wild, surely it looks an absolute mess, for the greater part of the year at least?

The truth is very different, as anyone will know whose spirits have been lifted by the sight of a brightly flowering buddleia covered in bees and butterflies sprouting from a crack in a grimy railway tunnel or by the fluorescent flicker of a dragon-fly across the barest stretch of water. A little touch of wilderness is subtle and surprising – it can delight or simply take the breath away. We can only marvel at nature's extraordinary persistence and fight for survival. Is this why we suddenly want to play our part? Does the recent enthusiasm for wildflower gardens and features result from an urge to help in the struggle to preserve the many plants and animals whose traditional habitats are daily under threat of destruction? Or is it that among today's bright

Fig 2   It can be fascinating to watch your garden re-establish some kind of ecological balance: a selection of natural plants will attract far more insects, which in their turn bring in the garden birds to feed their young.

Fig 3 (Opposite)   Your flower beds and borders can be given over to wilder species with spectacular results. Although not as showy as modern hybrids, wild flowers can still be stunners, such as the bright blooms and feathery foliage of Meconopsis.

Fig 4   Even a simple stone wall can provide an excellent natural habitat for wild plants and small creatures.

and busy but very stressful life-styles, we are only too eager to embrace our own little corner of peace and quiet. Somewhere unhurried and natural that cannot be fully controlled or made to conform, however small? Whatever your motives and the size of area you have available to dedicate to wildflower gardening, it is guaranteed to give you extreme pleasure in return for minimum maintenance; plus the satisfaction of knowing you are helping, even if it is in a very small way, to slow down the current ecological decline.

In the wild, flowers are wonderfully adapted to their habitat and, by approximating these conditions on whatever scale, you will, over a period of time, naturally generate a surprising range of plants, seemingly by magic. Waiting for your wild garden to develop spontaneously takes patience. However, with wildflower nurseries willing to

provide seeds and plants, or books like this one supplying the appropriate advice and information for raising your own plants, you can enjoy quicker – if not instant – results.

You will find that these natural habitats fall into several quite distinct environmental areas which can be adapted to garden features: flowers growing *en masse* in a patch or on an open sunny bank or border; lush and exotic water plants that you would find beside pond, stream and marsh; species that survive the barren conditions of rock and stone; and those shade-tolerant flowers that thrive in wood and hedgerow. As you will see from the feature ideas on the following pages, each of these groups offers vast scope for large and small design ideas that will not only provide a great deal of visual pleasure, but can enhance your general garden or patio plan. To look good, a wild or semi-wild feature must not only be

Fig 5 In the larger garden, a wild patch can look particularly effective if it merges with a backdrop of mature trees or a natural landscape beyond.

carefully thought out so that plants flourish, it must also be planned in relation to the rest of the garden so that it does not look incongruous. This can be done by careful landscaping, by blending several natural features and by linking to more formal features with areas of grass, rock or rustic paths. Incorporating herbs and old-fashioned cottage plants and features is a good way to blur the boundaries between wilder areas and the tamed formality of the modern garden.

Quite apart from the visual, relaxing and ecological advantages of using wild plants in the garden, they can serve another, very useful purpose. Because all these plants are specially adapted to difficult and extreme conditions: poor infertile soil, a boggy site or dense shade, they may be the ideal solution to a problem area: a ready-made group of differing heights, shapes, colours and forms which you can select to make a delightful feature of an otherwise wasted corner.

But you will not only be creating a miniature environment for a fascinating range of wild plants: you will also be re-creating the perfect habitat and food for many insects, birds, butterflies and small mammals. The range of wildlife your wildflower garden will attract even in an urban situation is amazing, especially if you are prepared not to be obsessively tidy and leave a few discreet piles of dead leaves, rotting branches and tangled undergrowth. Some are worth attracting simply for the enjoyment of observing them; others you will be helping to save from possible extinction.

Blossoms, fruits, seeds and berries will attract a wide range of birds by providing food through most of the months of the year; a good thick hedge and certain species of mature trees will encourage some to nest and you might also like to put up specially made bird boxes to encourage this. Water is an irresistible lure to a wide range of birds which would not normally be regular visitors to your garden, providing, of course, you incorporate some kind of shallows to enable them to go right down to bathe and drink.

Fig 6   One of the benefits of a wild garden is the greater range of birds and insects it will attract. An abundance of seeds and berries naturally brings many birds to feed, while a good thick hedge may even encourage certain species to nest and breed.

With wilder areas of the garden encouraging plenty of worms, beetles and other insects, plus a good range of different habitats, you may find you are also visited by a selection of nocturnal animal visitors, too: from tiny voles and mice to hedgehogs and even badgers looking for the seeds and insects, slugs and worms that are part of their regular diet. In time, you may also find your garden has become a haven for a fascinating collection of reptiles such as grass snakes, lizards and slow-worms — all harmless but fascinating to observe. A pond widens the scope further and will be quickly populated by frogs, toads and newts. You can encourage this yourself by introducing spawn.

A wildflower garden will naturally attract a large number of insects, and even if you are not mad about beetles, worms and hover-flies and your appreciation is limited to the sight of bumble-bees busy about your plants or dragon-flies hovering over the pool, you will surely enjoy the large number of birds that an insect-rich area will attract. Few can resist the sight of butterflies either, and the high nectar content of many wildflowers will turn your garden into a wonder-ful butterfly haven. Many plants, such as bud-dleia, hyssop, bugle and nettle, are particularly alluring to butterflies and you may see them literally smothered in these beautiful creatures when the flowers are in bloom. If you specifically

Fig 7 A well-planned wildflower garden has something of interest throughout the year. Few sights are lovelier in winter than the sparkle of snow on gold and russet foliage.

Fig 8   Herbs and wild flowers can turn your garden into a butterfly
haven. Try to leave a patch of nettles undisturbed to encourage the
pretty tortoiseshell to breed as this is what the caterpillars like to feed
on. Later, these charming brightly patterned butterflies will smother your
flowering plants.

Fig 9 A wild garden teaches you to look more closely at some of nature's wonderful forms in miniature: not just butterflies and tiny insects, but the plants themselves. This spectacular-looking bloom is, in fact, white clover (Trifolium repens) a common enough meadow flower but quite superb in close focus.

want to plan a butterfly garden, you should aim to provide food from early spring when flowers may be scarce, through to autumn and eventual hibernation. Butterflies are quite particular about where they will breed and some types have strict preferences as to which plants they like to lay their eggs or feed on. The holly blue, for example, likes to lay its eggs on and around holly plants; the orange tip prefers cuckoo flowers.

CHAPTER 2

Features Great and Small

From window-box to half-acre (0.2ha) field, whatever size of garden or patch you have decided to dedicate to a wildflower garden, the number of exciting ideas you can adopt or adapt to what you have available is almost infinite, providing you take into consideration the soil and climatic needs of the plants.

There are various factors that will determine the size of your wild garden. Obviously you are limited initially by the extent of plot you own, and this might range from a tiny town backyard to the average suburban back garden; or you may be lucky enough to enjoy a much larger country garden, perhaps even with the marvellous opportunity to buy extra land such as a field or piece of woodland. But while some of us are so keen on conservation and wildlife that we are prepared to turn the whole area we own over to

Fig 10 The range of shapes, colours and forms among natural wildflower species is certainly varied enough to create eye-catching combinations in your summer-flowering beds and borders.

Fig II Soft mauves, creams and whites are a major part of the
wildflower colour spectrum, the perfect foil for the green of long grass
and a contrast to the bright yellows. Common knapweed (Centaura
nigra) is particularly effective when planted en masse.

a natural wild garden with maybe a range of different features such as a small patch of meadowland, a bog or copse, most will be happy enough to dedicate just a corner or area of the main garden to wild plants and plan the remainder more conventionally. This can work very well and provide a great deal of fun and enjoyment, not just in creating a wildflower corner as a special feature, but also in observing the way it develops and the surprising range of wildlife it will attract, even in an urban setting.

When you have decided exactly how much space you are prepared to give over to controlled wilderness, you should then forget the limitations of its boundaries for a while. Your first consideration should be what kind of plants would be best suited to your chosen location: is it going to be dry and sunny, a damp boggy spot or a low shady area better suited to woodland plants? Even a tub or window-box will offer quite specific conditions that have to be borne in mind if your garden is to be a success. No plant flourishes in the wrong conditions and, while they can be rampant once established, wild plants can be particularly difficult to please with their sensitivity to the right ecological balance.

Chapters 3 to 7 describe in detail the different wildflower environments you can recreate within the confines of your garden and describe the wonderful variety of plants you might choose to suit each quite distinct area. Here we will look at just some of the individual and exciting ideas that could be created in today's gardens with this information at your fingertips. For further inspiration, just go out into the wild and study the wonderful blend of shapes and colours to be found in woodland, marsh or meadow while they still exist.

15

Fig 12   Mixing wild with more formal garden features can work if well planned. If you have the space, a flowery meadow might follow quite naturally from a closer-cropped, more conventional lawn.

LARGE FEATURES

Meadows

One of the features most people seem to want to reproduce for their personal pleasure is the wildflower meadow, and it is true that a level grassy area with a mass of different flowers and buzzing with insect life is among the loveliest wildflower features. It can also be one of the easiest to create and maintain. In fact, the area required to create this effect need not be that large: an area of only several yards (metres) square could be sufficient, and you could even sow a wildflower 'meadow' in a window-box (*see* page 23). But if you have the space, why not use it? Few sights, sounds and scents are more splendid than a meadow of softly blurred colours stretching before you. You can buy meadow grass and flower-seed mixtures from specialist wildflower and herb nurseries. For the best effects, it is important not just what you sow, but also when and how you cut your meadow. It must be cut by hand using a scythe either in July for a spring/early-summer-flowering meadow; or in autumn for a late summer meadow, to give the plants time to set seed.

Borders

If your garden is more formally laid out, you might consider dedicating one (or more) traditional, long flower borders to wilder species. Plant up with bulbs for spring – none of the fancy hybrid and double blooms and unusual colours but simple snowdrops, daffodils and crocus. Check the bulb catalogues for limited supplies of species bulbs, some of which, like the tulip species, can be quite exquisite. Then, in summer, plan for a succession of soft colours with clumps of yellow tormentil, blue-flowered bellflower or cushions of thrift's pink pompons. Because the majority of wild flowers tend to be smaller and less showy than our hybridized garden plants (there are exceptions: look at the magnificent teasel, growing over 6ft (2m) tall or the common poppy with its short-lived but wonderful blooms on slender stems), they look far more effective in drifts of subtle colour than planted individually. There is plenty of scope among the range of plants that enjoy the sunny conditions of the average border to satisfy all colour schemes.

Fig 13 The wildflower border is at its best in summer when plants are ideally displayed in clumps or groups of a single species to maximize the effect of their soft shapes and colours. Self-seeding in subsequent years will achieve this perfectly naturally.

Fig 14 Wilder elements can be introduced to great effect in the minimum of space: bordering an informal pathway or flight of garden steps, for example, where they will help soften any hard edges as well as provide a wonderful blend of soft shapes and colours.

17

Unless you are a ruthless weeder — and this is not really compatible with the principles of wildflower gardening — nature will take things into her own hands next year in any case. Most plants will self-seed, producing a totally different pattern to your lovely patchwork. This is half the fun of wildflower gardening — the element of unpredictability and surprise. If you would like some control over a large semi-formal border, you can mix wild flowers with other plants, providing you restrict yourself to the softer, more cottage-garden type of plant or flowering herbs so that they blend well and do not look out of place.

The same principles might be applied to a sunny island bed within a far more conventional garden to create a self-contained feature of

Fig 15 The effect of a fine creeping ivy on the trunk of a tree can make an eye-catching feature in its own right as well as an attractive element of the woodland garden.

special interest. For the best effect, remember that wild flowers grow to a wide variety of spreads and heights like any plants and that it makes sense to position taller species to the centre and low growers to the edges of your island bed. However, do not be disappointed if your wild subjects tend to be a bit wayward and position themselves where they please; you are not aiming at symmetrical perfection, after all.

Hedgerows

If you are looking for a large natural feature that will attract plenty of wildlife and serve a very practical purpose in the garden, why not create a wild hedgerow instead of a formal single-species hedge? This would look far more in keeping round a typical cottage or informal garden area and provides a great deal of pleasure in the variety of plants it can support as well as a wonderful range of small mammals and birds. Hedgerows are fast disappearing from our farming landscape with the introduction of larger fields, so this is a valuable contribution you could make to preserving part of the environment, too. Because a proper wild hedgerow is made up of a great many different species, you need plenty of space to create one successfully; this is also important as spreading roots and shade means little else will grow nearby. A wild hedgerow does need a little attention to keep it trimmed and free from weeds until established, but it is well worth it for the excellent variety of interest it can provide right through the year. Hawthorn, holly and blackthorn alone produce attractive flowers, foliage and berries through the seasons, for example. *See* pages 63–8 for more details on establishing a wild hedgerow.

Woodlands

If you have an area of garden with perhaps a couple of established trees, this can be converted into a delightful natural woodland garden, and you will not have to wait until the trees have grown to around 5ft (1.5m) tall. You may even be

Fig 16 Herbs and old-fashioned cottage flowers will complement the wildflower garden with their softer colours and informal shapes. A combination of such plants can also be useful to help integrate a wild garden with a more formal scheme.

lucky enough to have a larger patch of woodland that simply needs thinning and better under-tree planting. Alternatively, convert the whole of a dull and featureless suburban strip into a natural woodland walk with a careful selection of native trees and shade – and semi-shade-loving plants to smother the ground below. Your patience will eventually be well rewarded by a delightfully secluded, if unlikely, retreat that requires the absolute minimum of maintenance. All types of woodland are covered in detail on pages 52–62.

Ponds and Marshes

If, on the other hand, you want to see almost instant results, yet still create a large wildflower feature, you could plan an informal pond. This could be adapted to any size and rough shape that you wish, providing it receives adequate sunshine for plants to flourish and for the water not to become dank and stagnant. It is also not a good idea to site a pond directly beneath trees as falling leaves can be a real pollutant and a nuisance. Water-loving plants are among the most dramatic and lovely, and they tend to be

Fig 17   A drystone wall is the perfect habitat for a selection of creeping and trailing plants that will soften the stone with a lovely flowering curtain as well as protect the lizards, insects and other wildlife hiding within its cracks and crevices.

easy to grow and rampant spreaders so you should see results fairly quickly. Apart from the variety and excitement of water plants such as lilies, iris, rushes and reeds, even a modest-sized stretch of water will quickly attract a wide range of wildlife, such as frogs and toads, dragon-flies and birds.

If you are worried about the risk of young children around water in the garden, you may prefer to create a bog or marsh area (*see* pages 69–84 for creating all kinds of wild water gardens) where you can still grow an exciting selection of natural water's edge or marginal plants that enjoy a waterlogged soil, such as dramatic wild rhubarb with its huge leaves like parasols, bright flowering marsh marigolds or a beautiful blue spreading carpet of water forget-me-nots.

Rock-Gardens and Walls

Many gardeners love the scope and interest a rock or alpine garden offers and this can be a particularly lovely wildflower theme if you have a naturally raised and stony area or are planning to add height and interest to a more general scheme with a full-scale rockery. With the wildflower rock-garden in particular, it is important that the construction of the actual garden looks as natural as possible. It helps to use local stone and rock (cheaper, too) and to spend the time and trouble to get them arranged as naturally as possible. If local stone is unavailable or unsuitable for any reason, then weathered limestone tends to look most in keeping providing you remember that it will have a high alkali content and choose your plants accordingly. To get a feel for how it should look, you are recommended to go out and study in detail how rocks and boulders are laid down *in situ* in the wild to get the right effect.

You could also use a stone wall, or a level or raised gravel area to grow stony-site wild flower species such as maiden pinks, saxifrage and thrift if a full-scale rockery does not suit your plans. Most rock plants prefer a sunny situation, but be prepared to water regularly during dry spells as, while they like to be shallow rooted in poor soil, they do not enjoy completely drying out.

SMALL FEATURES

Flower-Beds and Corners

Plants, and wild plants in particular, are infinitely adaptable and most of the aforementioned ideas can be scaled down to suit small gardens or even areas with absolutely minimum facilities. A small raised bed of carefully chosen wild plants, according to whether it is sited in a sunny or shady location, is the small garden or patio's answer to the border or island bed with the advantage that it is also enclosed and kept relatively under control – although it should not look too neat and tidy as this will spoil the general effect. It is important to choose plants that will smother or semi-disguise the edges of your container. A natural timber or stone container would look best.

Simply a corner of the garden or patio might be dedicated to wildflower gardening by creating a tiny patch of meadowland, a marsh or pond. You could bravely let it encroach slightly on the main area by blurring the boundaries and letting it spread to join an informal path or stretch of lawn; or semi-enclose it in some way with screens or trellises of wild climbers such as honeysuckle or convolvulus, or with a wild hedgerow. The area immediately around a single established tree – frequently a gnarled old apple tree that no longer bears much fruit – makes an excellent small wild area if you treat it as the perfect environment for a selection of woodland shade-lovers. Choosing a selection of good ground-cover plants such as woodruff, green hellebore and sweet violet will not only provide an interesting display, but also clothe what is often a rather scruffy-looking area where little else will grow.

Fig 18 A small secluded corner of the garden could be designed to include a profusion of wilder, more natural plants and a simple seat to create a wonderfully relaxing retreat.

21

Fig 19 Simple schemes can be as effective as grand ones, and often the most successful ideas are simply making the most of existing garden features: here a wonderful old tree makes the ideal natural backdrop to wallflowers and other wild plants planted on top of a stone wall.

Tubs and Containers

The no-garden wildflower garden which is severely restricted in space and already totally paved, will have to take full advantage of tubs and containers. You can group them in a sunny position and plant them with a selection of grasses, wild herbs and smaller flowers like pansies and cornflowers; or plant pretty hedgerow crane's-bill, herb Robert or bugle if the area is unavoidably shady. Also consider softening the whole area by planting creeping plants like thyme between the cracks in paving slabs. You could even allow larger plants to flourish in this way if you want the area to have a semi-neglected wild atmosphere; most wild flowers are used to thin soil and difficult conditions.

Water can play its part as a small-scale wildflower feature, too. A natural pond or bog garden can be easily created in a tub or barrel, providing the container is waterproof, simply by filling it with water and planting it with a few water-loving plants. It is best to choose those with smaller flowers or foliage to keep in scale. Water plants tend to be rampant growers so you will have to keep an eye on them and trim them back if they threaten to grow too large.

Old sinks or troughs are marvellous for creating a compact alpine or rock-garden; you can disguise the shiny enamelled exterior by smearing it with adhesive and pressing on a mixture of sphagnum peat, sand and cement to roughen it up. Add a couple of inches (about 5cms) of pebbles or crocks in the bottom for drainage then a layer of turf or moss to prevent soil and water seeping through too quickly, and top up with a soil-based potting compost. A few rocks and boulders on the surface between your plants will create the best impression; plant up with small or creeping plants such as alpine lady's mantle, green and yellow roseroot, purple saxifrage, and wild thyme to soften the edges.

If you really have nothing more than a window-box, create your own little patch of wilderness with a few wild herbs or low-growing plants such as pansies, toadflax and primroses. You could even grow a miniature wildflower meadow in a window-box! In fact, any container, however small, can be adapted and planted with a suitable range of wild plants although reclaimed or rustic types tend to look more in keeping – old beer barrels, stone troughs, even hanging baskets. All will attract an amazing range of bees and butter-flies, however close to the city centre you live.

Lawns

If, like many people you do not have the room for a full-scale wildflower meadow, then why not instead plan a wildflower lawn? It will not resem-ble the usual smart arrangement of green stripes familiar as the traditional formal lawn in English gardens, but present a delightful display of but-tercups, daisies, dandelions and clover – all of which will probably appear quite naturally if you do not apply weed-killer or wield the mower just as they are coming up to bloom. Since lawns tend to be sited in fairly open, sunny situations, you could successfully add a scatter of other species: pretty blue speedwell, brilliant poppies or delicate pink ragged-robin.

For practical reasons, a wildflower lawn should not be sited in an area you will be passing through frequently or which needs to be kept regularly short. For, to allow your flowers to come to bloom, you must not cut it so

Fig 20 Lack of space or time need not rule out the chance to enjoy a wildflower feature. You can create a delightful wildflower alpine garden in miniature by planting up an old sink or trough with a few appropriate species and siting it on the patio or in a sunny corner of a small garden.

frequently. A single cut in March using the highest setting on your mower will be sufficient to keep it generally tidy and allow it to flower again later in the year, usually in late June. Then you can start cutting more regularly to keep it looking relatively trim.

Banks

A flowering bank can be any size and it might be fun to create one artificially using a small mound of soil (perhaps from a pool excavation) to add a little height and interest to a small back garden;

Fig 21 Use wild flowers to soften harder features around the house and garden. The ability of many species to survive with minimum soil and moisture means they can be grown successfully around stone, rock and concrete.

or a miniature mobile wildflower bank devised using a wooden framework and chicken wire filled with a suitable soil mixture to provide a screen or divider on the patio. This is vertical gardening at its best. Meadow plants will often do well on a bank providing they are species suited to poor, very well-drained soil. Lady's bedstraw grows well and is an attractive spreading plant with its fern-like foliage and yellow flowers. Fill your narrow frame with a good heavy compost and keep moist for a collection of damp meadow flowers like cowslips and ox-eye daisies. Many chalk-loving plants are also ideally suited to this kind of vertical arrangement; fill your frame or mound up with pure chalk with just a few inches (about five centimetres) of soil on top for planting one of the chalk-area flower and grass-seed mixtures available.

Miniature Woodlands

You might even have room for a miniature woodland, using shrubs and small deciduous trees rather than the traditional larger species to create a shady area for typical woodland ground-cover plants such as spring bulbs, primroses and rampant celandines. It all adds height and interest to what could be an otherwise bland garden; using natural plants is simply an added dimension.

If you are looking for something that will provide interest at eye level or to disguise the boundaries of a small plot in the prettiest, most natural way possible, take a look at some of the climbing wild flowers you might use. These generally grow fast and most have extremely attractive flowers and foliage that will quickly smother a frame, fence or trellis in the smallest garden or backyard. Sweet-scented honeysuckle is an obvious choice; also pretty pink dog roses with their mass of simple flowers. Two more vigorous natural climbers well worth growing are hop — choose a female plant if you want the papery flowers favoured by brewers (they will keep your house sweet smelling, too) — and traveller's joy, whose bright green leaves will

Fig 22 *Mosses, lichens and ferns will make a feature of an old stone wall. The maidenhair spleenwort* (Asplenium trichomanes) *has wonderfully delicate fronds that will sprout from the smallest crevice.*

quickly climb to a great height and which produces a most attractive fluffy mass of white flowers in late summer, giving it its alternative name of old man's beard.

Edgings

A relatively narrow border of wild plants can look lovely beside an informal path or flight of stone or timber garden steps. This is particularly suited to some shady area where rampant woodland ground-cover plants can be allowed to sprawl and semi-smother the edges.

25

CHAPTER 3

Meadows and Lawns

The combination of wild flowers in long grass is irresistible and one which can be adapted to any size of garden, or even a tub or trough. One of the easiest wild garden features to create and maintain, 'meadow mixtures' are available from specialist herb and wildflower nurseries and stockists – you may even find them at your local garden centre. Each contains a balanced mixture of grass and different wildflower species recommended for a particular soil type.

The traditional natural meadow is a wonderful sight, displaying as many as thirty different species of flowers in brilliant profusion over an area of only one square yard(metre); in a larger meadow of a couple of acres (a hectare), you might see over 150. While you cannot reproduce the effect of decades of ecological development, you can create a beautifully subtle patchwork effect and a wonderful haven for all kinds of wildlife. It is important that the area of land you are dedicating

Fig 23 A wildflower meadow will attract a wide range of fascinating wildlife from worms and moles to mice, frogs, grasshoppers and seed-loving birds such as goldfinches.

to your meadow is not too fertile. Poor thin soil, with either a sandy or lime bias, is ideal and this could be an excellent treatment for such an area where you can do little else with it without expensive and extensive enriching of the soil. The reason for this is that grasses will flourish too well in rich soil and outstrip your flowers. You can reduce its fertility if necessary by stripping off the turf and around 4in (5–10cm) of topsoil, depending on soil type and depth. Do not throw that valuable topsoil away – use it somewhere else in the garden.

Fig 24 *Even a humble unsprayed roadside will reveal the wonderful colour-spangled effect of wildflowers growing naturally in long, rough grass.*

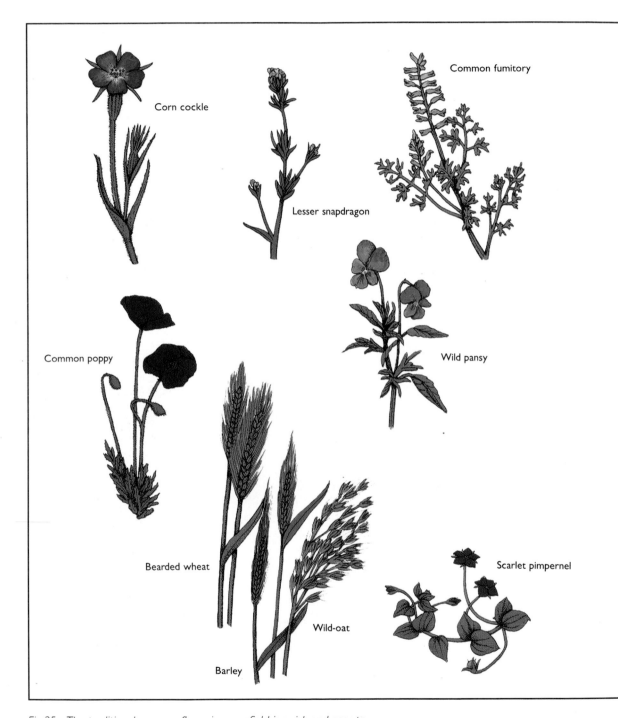

Fig 25   The traditional summer-flowering cornfield is quick and easy to reproduce on any scale from field to window-box, if you choose the right plants, such as corn marigolds, poppies, barley and scented mayweed.

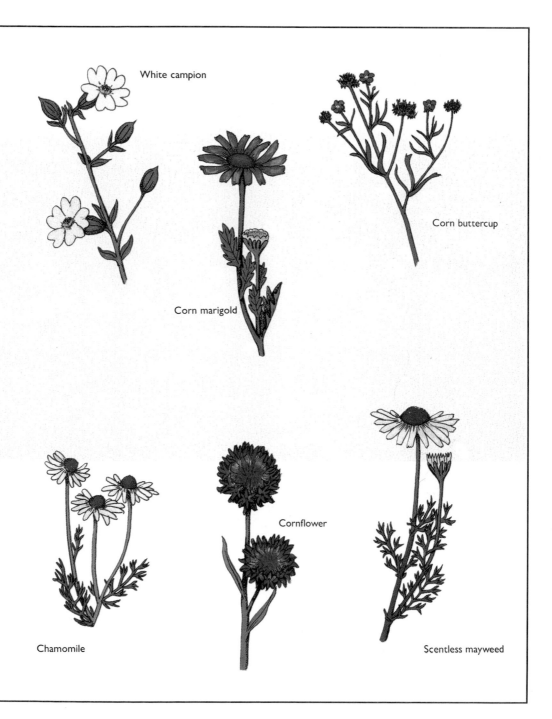

White campion

Corn buttercup

Corn marigold

Chamomile

Cornflower

Scentless mayweed

Fig 26   The familiar meadow in full flower: traditional buttercups and daisies make a wonderful sight en masse.

Equally important is the need to eradicate all perennial weeds, such as thistle and dock, either by hand-weeding and digging out all the roots; or, if the area is large, you may consider using a perennial non-persistent weed-killer. If you do not like using chemicals and have the time and patience, there is an alternative. You must mow the area as closely as possible over several seasons using a grass box and making sure you rake up all the clippings.

Different seed mixtures are available to suit various soil types. You should also consider whether the site is in a sunny or shady position and look at the proximity of other features. A stretch of meadowland may look out of place beside a very formal layout, for example. It would be much better to position it close by a hedge or cluster of trees to extend the idea of a natural landscape; or to link it to other wild plant features such as a pond or marsh.

You could create a flowery meadow that blooms for most of the year, but much easier to organize and maintain is either a spring- or summer-flowering area of grass. Alternatively, you could designate two areas to come to flower in succession; perhaps a spring-flowering lawn beneath a deciduous tree, designed to bloom before the tree bursts into leaf and overshadows it; and an adjoining summer-flowering meadow in a more open, sunny patch. You can create

Fig 27 Bulbs should be planted in swathes or drifts in areas of long grass
for the most natural effect. Flowers should naturalize and multiply each
year to produce a spectacular spring display.

paths through large areas of longer, flowering grass by regularly mowing a strip to the width of your mower – gently winding rather than a straight passage will look more natural. Or a conventionally tended band of grass such as this can be used to divide a wildflower area from a more formal part of the garden.

Fig 28   Despite its delicate yellow flowers, the mountain pansy (Viola lutea) is a tough creeping plant, creating a low mat of foliage in poor soil and tolerating even very dry stony ground.

CREATING A MEADOW FROM SCRATCH

When you have impoverished the soil by removing the turf and fertile topsoil, it should be dug over and well raked, and then rolled to provide a fine seed-bed. This should only be attempted in dry weather as a damp clogged soil will make your job impossible. Take your chosen meadow-seed mix – for spring or autumn flowering and the correct soil type – and broadcast it at a rate of around 1oz (3–4g) per square yard (metre); mixing the seed with fine sand makes it easier to spread evenly. You should toss half the seed in one direction, then half in the other. The best time to sow is in autumn if you can, as this gives

Fig 29   Pot-grown plants can be introduced to an existing grass area by digging out a hole slightly larger than required, gently inserting the plant so that it is level with the surrounding turf, back-filling and firming down.

Fig 30 Geranium pratense alba *is a lovely white form of the meadow crane's-bill, featuring the same attractive foliage but white instead of the familiar wide-open blue-purple blooms.*

Fig 31 *Before you sow wildflower seed into an existing area of grass, it must be vigorously raked or 'scarified' to expose patches of bare soil.*

the seeds a winter to prepare them for growing naturally; this may encourage faster germination. However, if this is impossible, sow in early spring.

You may make up your own mixture by selecting the seed of the individual plants you want to grow and mixing them with a non-rye grass mix. Recommended grasses include: quaking grass (*Brizia media*), meadow foxtail (*Alopecurus pratensis*) and annual meadow grass (*Poa annua*). Seeds should be watered using a fine rose.

You should cut the area to a height of around 2–4in(5–10cm) every six to eight weeks during the first year to prevent the grass taking over and to encourage your flowers to make good root growth; you should not expect any flowers until the following year.

CREATING A MEADOW IN AN EXISTING LAWN

You can transform an existing lawn into a wildflower meadow. Decide whether you want a spring- or autumn-flowering meadow, as this will influence the plant varieties you choose. Stop applying fertilizer and reduce fertility by lifting the turfs and removing a layer of the richer topsoil as described on page 32. There are a couple of ways you could successfully introduce wild flowers into the grass. The first involves cutting the lawn as closely as possible in either early spring or autumn and raking vigorously to remove any loose grass. This should also produce patches of bare soil in which you can sow your wildflower seed. This is done by raking in the seed on a good dry day, then rolling to compact. Water lightly after sowing as you would for grass seed.

Fig 32   If you have the space, it is worth dedicating a large area to creating a wildflower meadow, as it blends well with other features and can successfully be married with more conventional shorter turf and lawn areas.

You will have to cut the area every six to eight weeks during the first year using the mower blade set high, ideally leaving growth about 3–4in (7–10cm) tall. This will not harm your wild flowers – in fact, it should actually encourage root growth – but it will discourage the grass from taking over. It is important to remove all the clippings.

The alternative is to clear areas of grass by hand and introduce pot-grown wild flowers into the lawn. This is a good option for smaller areas where you would only require a small amount of seed or where you do not want to wait for what might be a long germination period for some species. You can grow the plants yourself from seed as described on page 85, or buy the plants from a specialist nursery. To give the plant the best possible chance, water both the pot and the ground before planting. Lift the plant out of the pot gently without damaging stem or roots, then dig a hole just a bit wider and deeper than the root ball of the plant. Place the plant in the hole to check that the plant is at the same level in the turf as it was in the soil of its pot, then back-fill, taking care to spread out any roots gently and keeping the plant upright. Firm well at the top to prevent air gaps or subsidence, and water in thoroughly.

Fig 33 Conservation bodies have experimented successfully with lifting sections of threatened, established flowering turf and transferring it to a new site. This idea could be adapted to your own garden if you know someone who already has a flowering meadow or lawn. You should never lift plants from the wild.

Fig 34 It is important to rake up the hay after cutting a wildflower meadow or grass area to prevent it mulching down and encouraging unwelcome, vigorous plants to flourish and take over.

MOWING YOUR MEADOW

Correct mowing is essential to the success of a wildflower meadow, and the right technique depends on whether you have created a spring- or summer-flowering feature. You will not be able to use your regular cylinder mower for what is strictly speaking hay making; a hand scythe is the best and traditional method, but hard work, especially if the area is quite large. Small areas could be cut by motorized strimmer, but a wheeled rotary motor is probably the best labour-saving option since the blades can be set at different levels.

Spring Meadow Mowing

If you have planned a spring-flowering meadow, the grass should be left unmown until summer – around June or July, which, depending on location and weather, should give your wild flowers time to bloom and set seed for next year. Scythe or mow to a height of around 2–4in (5–10cm) and leave the hay where it falls to dry for a couple of days. You could put it to good use for animal bedding or fodder if you turn it over with a fork to aerate it in the sun to make hay; this would also encourage any loose seeds to fall. Rake up and remove when dry. You can now mow as you normally would your lawn – probably weekly unless the weather is unnaturally hot and dry – but making sure you remove all grass cuttings. You can use the area as a normal lawn but take care that you do not mow too close; remember not to use any fertilizer either.

Summer Meadow Mowing

For a summer-flowering meadow, you should be mowing or scything regularly from early spring until early summer, taking care not to mow too closely. Do not mow until autumn when the flowers have bloomed and dispersed their seed. Cut, dry and remove as described above.

With both spring- and summer-flowering meadows, it is a good idea to trample it after the main mow of the year to press the seed into the soil – a job normally done by grazing cattle.

Meadow Management to Encourage Wildlife

If you are keen to encourage butterflies to breed and feed on your meadow area, you will have to tackle it slightly differently. The larger the area, the greater the variety of species you will attract; but even a small area will support a large number of maybe one or two types which will be a pleasure to observe. Each has a particular preference as to habitat: some like a short turf,

Fig 35 Always a cheerful sight, large ox-eye daisies (Leucanthemum vulgare) are a natural lure to butterflies and other meadow insects.

others a longer grass or particular plant species, so you may like to incorporate a variety of environments. Other areas could be mown at random and differing times to produce areas of long and medium grass. A final cut all over in autumn should keep the area under general control.

MAKING A FLOWER LAWN

If you simply like the idea of flowers blooming in your lawn but do not particularly want to go to the trouble of creating an authentic meadow, you could simply encourage wild plants to grow naturally by not mowing until summer. This will only work if you have not applied weed-killer for the last couple of years and it is surprising the variety of flowers that will bloom even in the first year. Daisies, dandelions, clover, self-heal, speedwell and cow parsley may all appear. Begin normal mowing after the flowers have finished.

Fig 36 The unmistakable golden 'keys' of the lovely cowslip, now sadly disappearing from the wild but, thanks to availability of cultivated plants and seed, still a charming sight in spring as part of the wildflower garden.

Another quick and easy way to have your lawn flowering through spring is to plant swathes of spring-flowering bulbs in the grass. Use the more natural varieties rather than showy hybrids and plant in wide groups or bands – never in small clumps of maybe one or two bulbs – to make planting and mowing easier. It looks more effective, too, to have blocks of colour amongst the grass. To get the most natural effect, you should toss them gently towards the area where you want them planted and simply put in to a depth of around four times their size wherever they land. This produces a random effect and avoids any straight lines. The quickest way to plant a lot of bulbs is using a special tool; alternatively, remove a section of turf, plant a few bulbs, then replace. The bulbs should naturalize and spread to create an even more abundant and natural look in future years. To encourage this, you should allow the foliage to die back naturally and the flowers to set seed so that the bulb will bloom again. Grass should ideally be left un-mown until early summer, so bear this in mind when planning your planted areas. After this, the lawn can be mown as usual.

MAKING AN ANNUAL WILDFLOWER MEADOW OR CORNFIELD

One of the quickest and most satisfying wildflower features you can create in your own garden is an approximation of the wonderful

Fig 37 The smallest patch of grass can be seeded with a few summer-flowering wild flowers and planted with several clumps of spring bulbs to create an informal effect in the minimum of space.

Fig 38   Spreading quickly and readily from seed or cuttings, self-heal
(Prunella vulgaris) produces a patch of rich purple in long grass and is an
excellent bee and butterfly plant.

spread of flowering weeds that once plagued the farmer's fields of wheat and barley. As well as a wonderful visual experience, it can be exciting to re-create something no longer seen owing to modern herbicides. Like meadow seed, you can buy special cornfield mixes; add a handful of wheat and barley seed for a really authentic effect. Again, this could be adapted to any size of feature, although it would not be such a good idea if your garden borders grain fields. You will not be popular with the farmer if your flower seeds spread as they are sure to do. On the other hand, his chemical sprays may well drift into your garden and destroy your own plans. You do not have to worry about poor soil conditions to sow a flowering cornfield as you will not be planting competitive grasses, but you must always cultivate or disturb the soil in some way in spring and autumn in order to encourage the natural germination of seeds. Sowing in autumn should produce results early the following summer; if you would like to delay flowering until mid- or late summer, you should, however, sow in early spring.

CHAPTER 4

Sunny Banks and Borders

BORDERS

Your traditional herbaceous border can easily be converted into a delightfully informal wildflower version, especially if it is in a good sunny site and the rest of the garden (if small) is not too formal by contrast. In the larger garden, you could perhaps create a wildflower border as part of an informal, natural corner and incorporate a meadow or pond area, too. The border may not be as difficult to control and keep looking good as you might imagine, especially if you combine your wildflower planting with a framework of small trees, shrubs and maybe ornamental, but not too showy, garden plants.

It may be a good idea to introduce just a few wild flowers your first year, and gradually increase the number of varieties to build up the picture

Fig 39   Wilder species look best grown in large clumps and allowed to mingle informally.

Fig 40 Mix old-fashioned cottage plants and wild flowers to create a superb flowering border. This striking scheme has cleverly been kept in check by the deep green of a formal lawn to the fore and a semi-formal hedge as a backdrop.

as you become more confident or fresh species suggest themselves. The idea, right from the beginning, is to leave no bare patches. Less bare soil not only looks more attractive and con-tributes to the natural effect of some kind of semi-wild profusion, but also keeps maintenance to a minimum by reducing the need to water and weed. You will probably want to be selective

41

Fig 41   The maiden pink (Dianthus deltoides) *is an easy-to-grow, spreading plant that will flourish at the base of your borders along gravel paths. The flowers are small but a brilliant rose-red colour which attracts plenty of insects.*

with your weeding, allowing some of the more attractive species to grow and add to the effect. You should not let this get out of hand, however; you want the garden to look natural but not a tangled mess. Gaps between young shrubs and perennial plants can be temporarily filled with quick-growing annuals if necessary.

If a long border does not fit the shape of your garden, consider applying the same principles to an island bed or even a raised bed on the patio where a semi-wild area would look appropriate. The recommended principles of planning a bed or border still apply; tall plants to the rear or centre; smaller plants to the fore. But, in this case, you should only apply these rules as a rough guide. They are particularly appropriate to your backbone planting which hopefully is not going to change places as the years pass.

Wilder plants, on the other hand, have a habit of doing their own thing, particularly when they start to self-seed, producing a more random and attractive effect. You should also remember that wild flowers look better *en masse* so do not restrict their areas to too small a patch. Sow or plant plenty of them and do not be afraid to let them spread themselves a bit to get the best effect – you should be aiming at drifts of a single colour amongst the greenery.

You are also relieved to some extent from the burden of detailed colour planning as the softer shades and simpler shapes of wild flowers tend to blend well together, even when traditionally the colours are contrasting and should clash. That said, you will find plenty of scope in both

Fig 42 (Opposite)   *The subtle effect of growing herbs and wild flowers in the traditional border: a relaxing blend of greens, creams and yellows and a wonderful variety of foliage shapes with a tall, handsome fennel plant taking pride of place to the rear.*

Fig 43   A wildflower border will attract a wonderful number of bees and butterflies seeking pollen and nectar to add to your own enjoyment and to the value of your garden as an environmental refuge.

heights and colours from the tall foxgloves and thistles – with wonderfully contrasting flower heads but such complementary colours – to the lower, spreading greater knapweed which produces a mass of spidery red flowers in summer among feathery green foliage. This is a plant that will tolerate semi-shade so can be grown in the shadow of larger plants and shrubs.

If you are looking for a stunner, poppies always oblige and grow easily, self-seeding to produce an increasingly spectacular display year after year until you choose to thin them out. If you like the sunny effect of yellow, choose sun-loving yellow rattle, the tall flower spikes of dark mullein; or common toadflax – not so common to look at with its clusters of flowers like tiny snapdragons.

You will find plenty of mauves and pinks among the wildflower species, too; not just familiar harebells and cornflowers. But also pretty pink musk mallow, pink- or mauve-flowered self-heal which acts like a magnet to bees and butterflies, or the stunning fritillary, surely one of the most exotic wild flowers with its hanging blooms featuring eye-catching blotched markings. One plant that grows extremely well and makes a wonderful display is meadow crane's-bill, such an excellent plant that it is perhaps now seen more often in cottage gardens than in the wild. It makes a dense clump of attractive divided foliage and a mass of mauve/blue flowers. It spreads readily from year to year and makes good ground cover.

It is where you might be adding more ornamental species that you should be careful, by choosing the more subtle varieties and keeping to single or dual colour themes to highlight your wild flowers, such as soft blues and mauves, pale pinks and lilacs or creams and pale yellows. Old-

Fig 44 Informal paths of stone, brick or bark chips are invaluable for defining your wildflower features and separating flowering borders and areas of long grass from other, maybe more formal, parts of the garden.

Fig 45 Even those with nothing more than a concrete backyard can enjoy a wildflower oasis by arranging the plants in containers, such as old barrels. Plant up pots of a single species or create lovely blends of soft colours and shapes.

fashioned cottage flowers and herbs are always a good choice, for while they are still easy and reliable to grow, they tend to look far softer and more modest than their modern hybrid cousins. Your backbone planting can be a clever blend of different greens, highlighted by seasonal flowers and berries – again, nothing too showy. The range of shrubs, small trees, ferns and other foliage plants available should provide scope for all heights, spreads and effects. In this way you can plan for year-round interest, too, which is always a problem with essentially spring- and summer-flowering wild flowers. This continuity is to advantage of the wildlife you will be attracting, too, providing a wider range of food and habitats throughout the seasons.

Do not be tempted to try to give your plants a boost in the wildflower border by applying fertilizer. A reasonable soil will be sufficient, and enriching it may cause all kinds of problems –

it may eradicate the plant altogether, produce lush growth of foliage but no flowers, or simply encourage pests. If you do have problems with pests or disease, also stay your hand from the chemical cures. Many are too strong and will kill your plant as well as the problem; a good wildflower garden should attract plenty of natural predators in any case.

WILD FLOWERS FOR SUNNY SLOPES

Wild plants naturally grow well up an incline or bank and there is no reason why you should not exploit this decorative tendency to create a semi-vertical feature instead of, or as well as, a flower border. If you have an existing grassy bank, plant it up with flowers using one of the techniques described for meadows or lawns (see page 26).

Fig 46   Remarkably good natured in that it tolerates sun or semi-shade, honesty (Lunaria annua) makes a rich display of colour in summer and pretty clusters of flat seed pods popular with flower arrangers at the end of the season. It self-seeds easily and is an excellent choice for the butterfly border.

Any of the meadow-flower varieties that like a well-drained soil should do well: lady's bedstraw will spread quickly and produces a lovely mass of tiny yellow flowers; low-growing common bird's-foot-trefoil with its delicate blooms will also flourish in poor, well-drained soil. The advantage of growing one of the meadow-grass and flower mixtures on a bank is that poor soil and free draining will ensure that the grasses do not grow so vigorously, allowing the flowers a better chance to establish themselves, and will probably need cutting only once a year.

You could build a grassy bank from scratch, especially if you have a natural rise or a mound of soil to dispose of, and plan for a range of plants from spring-flowering cowslips to summer's rampant wild clover, vigorous creeping tufted vetch and bright-eyed yellow and white ox-eye daisies.

It makes a useful landscaping feature as part of a larger wild garden, too, as a boundary or backdrop.

A chalk bank – ideal for a great many wildflower species – is even easier to build. It should face full sun and be no higher than 3ft (90cm); do not make it too steep or it will look unnatural. Chalk rubble is best to use for the actual construction. Tread it down so that it makes a compact seed-bed. If you choose your plants carefully you can sow them directly into the chalk – there is no need for any soil. You can buy grass and flower mixtures specially formulated for chalk and which may include perennial flax, tiny-leaved salad burnet, sweet-scented wild thyme and feathery wild carrot with its flat white flower heads, really a cluster of tiny individual flowers; all are best are best sown in autumn.

Fig 47   In the larger garden, a wildflower border can create a wide, informal band on either side of a meandering path and may be allowed to merge into shrubbery or woodland behind.

ROCK, STONE AND BRICK

A variation of this idea is the rock or wall wildflower garden. Again, there are many varieties specially suited to the sunny conditions and poor, thin soil of a stony terrain. Also, the extra height of a feature like this could be useful in a garden of any size to add variety or create a natural-looking boundary. You do not have to build a major construction, which may look out of place in any case: a modest mound, a wall or even an area of gravel will provide the ideal environment for these plants and may suit your scheme better. If the only space you have is the patio, plant between the slabs with sweet-smelling wild flowers and herbs like the low-growing Treneague chamomile or different thymes and marjorams. You can create your rock garden in an old stone sink (*see* page 22).

Fig 49   Red valerian (Centranthus ruber) likes a sunny position and stony soil, producing a mass of large, red scented blooms that are very attractive to butterflies.

Fig 48   Thrift or sea-pink (Armeria maritima) is another tough but very attractive flowering plant ideal for banks and borders. It thrives in a sunny position to create a dense mat of spiky green foliage and bright pink pompon blooms.

Wild alpines prefer sun and good drainage but they do need plenty of rainfall as well, so you will have to water during dry spells; covering any areas of bare soil with stone chippings will help to conserve moisture. You will find an interesting range of suggestions for rocky wildflower features suiting all sizes of garden on pages 20 and 22. Even a simple pile of rubble can be converted into a pretty scree garden for displaying creeping wild thyme or *Alchemille alpina* (the eye-catching alpine lady's mantle, with its glossy leaves and tiny green-yellow flower clusters that always look so fresh and appealing, is ideal for a dull corner).

An old brick or stone wall can also make a splendid environment for wild plants, and a wide variety of wildlife will also love all those cracks and crevices. You can insert soil into any cracks to encourage plants to grow. A drystone wall looks the most natural, especially if you are building from scratch; but this is not as easy to construct as it looks; you will need expert assistance if it is to last. A well-built wall should last for years and support a wide range of pretty flowering plants. The plants not only provide a fine display but will also soften the outlines of the wall. This can be even more important where the wall is made of brick and you want to create a fairly natural, wild effect. The appearance of old weathered brick helps, and if you have to build a new brick wall it is worth trying to get hold of second-hand bricks for more matured look.

There are a great many lovely wild alpines you can choose from to plant up your rock, brick or

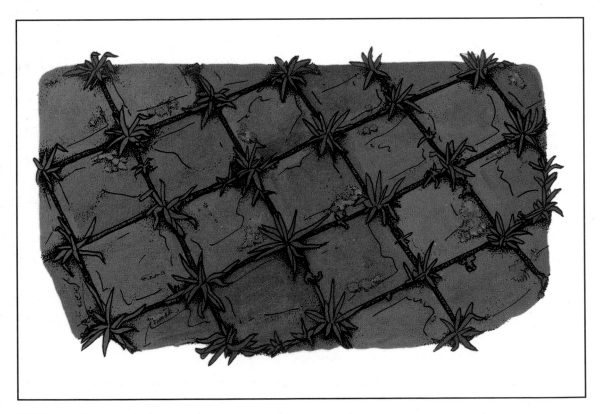

Fig 50 Even if your garden has been completely paved over, you might successfully insert wildflower plants in the cracks between the paving on courtyard or patio.

Fig 51 With its unusual fleshy stems and bright yellow starry flowers, wall-pepper (Sedum acre) will make a feature of an old stone wall.

stone feature; one of the most beautiful is roseroot – a sedum producing rosettes of fleshy leaves and fluffy-looking yellow flower-heads irresistible to bees and butterflies. Far more delicate but equally stunning is the mountain avens (*Dryas octopetala*) which clings close to the stone with tiny, almost feathery, evergreen leaves and bright white-petalled flowers with dusted yellow centres. In the wild it often chooses to nestle between slabs of limestone pavement.

51

CHAPTER 5

Woodland and Shade

The beauty of wild flowers is that the majority are specially adapted to difficult conditions so they can be usefully employed in those problem areas of the garden to create an attractive and

Fig 52   The well-planned woodland or any tree-planted area provides something of interest at every level; from the lofty tree tops down to ground cover. Here bright honesty (Luneria annua) provides foreground interest against a leafy backdrop of leaves and branches.

successful feature. One of the trickiest environments to deal with is deep or partial shade, but for wild woodland plants these conditions are ideal. Some are suited to full shade, others to a dappled or semi-shade. But if you have an area shaded by trees and shrubs, or, as is common in town and city gardens, a garden or patio shaded by tall walls or surrounding buildings, careful selection of some of these species will provide the ideal solution and the pleasure of some fascinating and beautiful plants. It may be that you wish to create a natural shady area anyway and that you will be looking for suitable trees and shrubs to create a miniature (or larger) woodland effect within your garden.

Before you get carried away with enthusiasm, you must appreciate that you will need patience; there are no short cuts and a successful woodland area can take several decades to achieve the look you are aiming at. However, the lovely flowers that clothe the woodland floor are much faster grower — some, like the waxy yellow-flowered celandine, can be annoyingly invasive — and you can plan a succession of species, not just to provide interest from season to season, but also to match the gradually developing shade above.

CHOOSING TREES AND SHRUBS

For the most natural effect, you must choose native tree species. Unless you are planning an area of more than half an acre (0.2ha), it is also advisable to select the smaller types such as alder, birch, elderberry, holly, hazel, rowan and

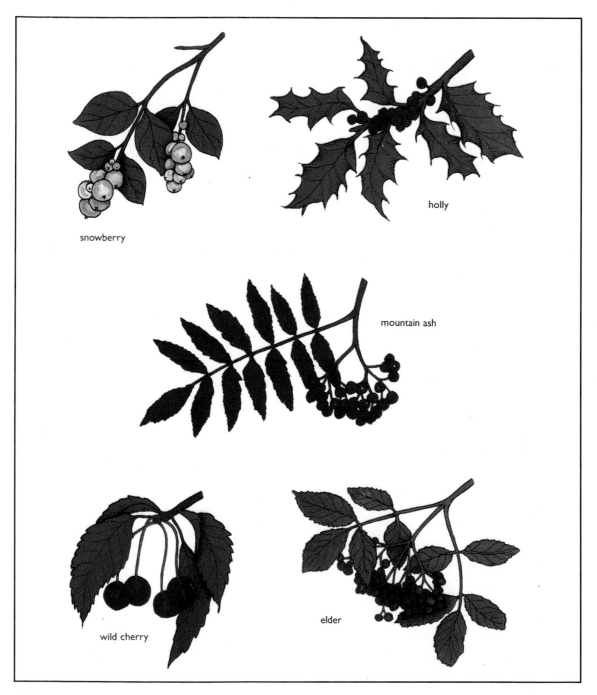

snowberry

holly

mountain ash

wild cherry

elder

Fig 53 One of the pleasures of growing trees and shrubs in the garden is the year-round interest they can provide – not just their general shape and the freshness of the leaves, but also the wonderful spring blossom and, later, autumn fruits and berries that will attract many insects and birds.

53

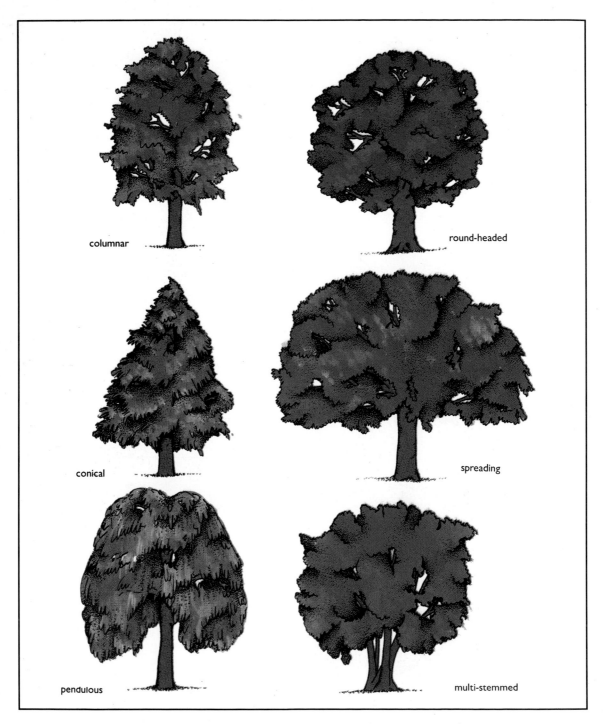

Fig 54 Trees and shrubs grow naturally into a range of different shapes
that can be used to add variety to your woodland scheme.

thorn. You should resist the showier ornamental hybrids as these create too artificial a look. These are more effective anyway when used singly or in small groups of a single species among more modest types to get maximum impact from their unusual or striking characteristics. You will find that a selection of smaller trees planted close together will do better than a couple of large trees.

When deciding which species to choose, the pattern of native trees changes drastically from region to region and according to soil type, so it may help to study the natural variety of species in your particular area. Thus, you will no doubt discover acers and hornbeams growing on heavy clay soils; willows and poplars in damp wetlands;

Fig 56   This white-flowered form of daphne, Daphne mezereum 'Alba', has yellow fruits.

Fig 55   The elder tree, Sambucus nigra, *is excellent value for smaller gardens, providing virtually year-round interest with attractive blossoms in spring and clusters of dark berries in autumn.*

and beech, birch and hawthorn flourishing on the freer-draining chalky uplands. As a general guide, you will want a blend of different trees that look well together, with not too many surprises such as those with deep bronze or striking yellow foliage.

You will find a wonderful variety of tree and leaf shapes to play with without worrying about a limited colour scheme of different shades of green, which looks delightful and just right in a natural woodland setting anyway. Trees can be

55

Fig 57   When planning a woodland area, however small, you should apply the principle of a multi-layered effect including a high canopy of tall trees, graduating down through smaller trees and shrubs to the shade-loving plants of the woodland floor.

tall, thin and erect (called columnar) – a good choice for areas with limited space; round-headed where a ball of foliage spreads itself above a single straight trunk or stem; conical, resulting in the tree tapering almost to a point at its top; or pendulous, producing an attractive arched effect that looks particularly good beside water where it creates interesting reflections. Looking closer – for like water a woodland or area of trees is always a place where you are encouraged to sit and linger and enjoy your surroundings – foliage variety ranges from round and oval leaves, palm shapes and hearts to deeply divided pinnate forms, arrowheads, feathery fern-like foliage and needle-thin leaves.

The best effect, depending on the size of feature you are planning, is to arrange your trees in groups of at least three or five; odd numbers look best and avoid too regular or artificial an effect. These should be at least 3–5ft (1–1.5m) apart to encourage good growth and branch shape, yet exclude sufficient light to suppress any weeds below. The most natural effect is achieved if you choose a selection of trees of varying heights (taller species can be coppiced if they grow too tall), graduated down to shrubs to create a natural three-dimensional layered effect. You should be aiming at a 'high canopy' of your tallest trees: these are the ones that will receive most light but create most shade below. Beneath these is the 'understorey' of smaller shade-tolerant species and large shrubs, and then a 'brush' layer of the smaller shrubs and creepers. Finally, where light and space permits, there are the herbaceous plants on the woodland floor, many of which survive by establishing themselves each year before the deciduous leaf cover above develops and creates deep shade.

The Canopy

The space available and the effect you are hoping to achieve will influence the number and type of trees you choose and how they are positioned. In the small suburban garden, you will probably be hoping to create a more intimate, wild effect, and your trees may well be required to hide some eyesore or evidence of surrounding habitation. Around the perimeters, columnar or conical evergreens, such as Irish yew and holly, can be grown close together if you need dense all-year screening. Alternatively, walls and fences can be successfully smothered in woodland climbers such as honeysuckle, white bryony and traveller's joy. However small a garden you have, you should still follow the principles of a natural woodland within your main planting scheme, as described above: a blend of light and shade, tall trees and smaller species, with shrubs and herbaceous ground cover below. Remember to create logical paths and clearings, even if your garden is on a very small scale, to allow access and enjoyment of both your trees and the wild flowers below. In a very small garden it may be good idea to prune off the lower branches every year to make more space beneath and between – to a height of about 4–5ft (1.2–1.5m) should be sufficient. This should be carried out while the tree is dormant between the end of autumn and beginning of spring.

If planning and planting a larger garden or small copse, you can plan a greater variety of trees, planted close together to produce a denser

Fig 58 The woodland floor can be as fascinating as the variety of trees and shrubs that shade it. Here the unusual and highly poisonous orange berries of lords and ladies (Arum maculatum) rise glistening on a long stalk above a mulch of dead leaves and creeping ivy.

effect and incorporating glades and clearings. Try to include at least one or two evergreen species and one with interesting autumn colour for year-round interest. There is always a temptation to plant too many trees; yours might need thinning out after a couple of years. Select the weakest trees and fell or coppice, leaving the others to grow stronger and allowing more light to reach the woodland floor.

The Understorey

Shrubs and the smaller trees that form the understorey need to be chosen with particular care because, until the high canopy matures, they are going to provide the main area of interest and shade for your woodland plants. They should ideally be planted close enough for their branches eventually to intertwine – separate

Fig 59 A small woodland is one of the easiest features to merge with a more formal garden: it might form a backdrop or boundary, or be approached by an informal path, more formal plants gradually giving way to wilder species.

shapes are for conventional, more formal gardens. At the edges of your tree area, flowering and fruiting ramblers such as rose and bramble are particularly useful: they grow quickly and look wild and natural, with the added bonus of pretty blooms and fruits to attract a wide range of wildlife.

The Woodland Floor

A single established tree in a small garden can also be successfully underplanted to create a miniature woodland area. Despite the deep shade which usually discourages anything from growing, leaving an ugly patch of bare soil, natural woodland plant species, such as woodruff with its glossy green leaves and tiny white flowers, primrose, violet and ground ivy, will all flourish and cover the ground right up to the stem. If the tree is large and the shade very dense, you may be restricted to lily-of-the-valley, wood avens and cyclamen – no disadvantage as these are superb flowering plants.

If you like this compact woodland idea but have no suitable trees in your garden, you may have the patience to plant the tree, too; silver birch is a good choice as it is relatively fast growing, has attractive bark, foliage and general shape. Alternatively, consider a rowan with its lovely autumn colour and berries and fresh spring foliage – a good-value feature tree for small gardens; a bird cherry; or hawthorn, again a small easy-to-grow tree with the advantage of spring, summer and autumn interest.

PLANTING UP THE WOODLAND EDGE

Once your trees become established and a good mulch builds up below, wild seeds will begin to germinate to create a woodland edge environment. You can plant wild flowers along the borders of your tree planting; or create a sunny clearing – a natural glade effect. You may be surprised at the variety of species that will tolerate

Fig 60 *Exotic-looking cyclamen thrive in the shady conditions beneath trees and shrubs where little else will survive.*

these shady or semi-shady conditions, but you only have to walk through a woodland with your eyes to the ground at any time of year to see the delicate beauty – and vigour – of many flowering varieties. The majority are perennial or biennial plants which spread or grow well and so are very easy to look after once established.

Unlike the meadow flowers, most are used to the rich fertile mulch of the woodland floor. Mulching with organic matter for the first couple of years is a good idea until fallen leaves, bark and other debris within your tree area establish their own balance. Mulching not only provides nutrition but also suppresses unwelcome weeds – so no spraying is necessary – and will conserve water. One of the best forms of mulch are wood chips, which not only look completely natural but will start to establish the right kind of fungi and bacteria.

A great many woodland plants like moist conditions, too – incidentally, making them ideal for a dank shady corner of the patio or that difficult area beside the front door. These are also wild plants useful for the edges of established **areas of** trees and shrubberies if you are keen to establish an almost instant woodland edge effect or have found this a difficult spot to plant successfully. Ferns are wonderful for providing a range of exciting foliage effects; from the classic male fern:

Fig 61 Woodland wild flowers and foliage plants are perfect for those awkward shady corners in the town garden, where they can be used to create a superb lush effect.

(*Dryopteris filix-mas*) with its fresh ferny green fronds to the long tongues of the aptly named hart's tongue fern (*Phyllitis scolopendrium*). Flowers can be chosen virtually all year round from the first snowdrops pushing their heads up through the snow, followed by sweet violets and green hellebore in early spring. Later there are bluebells and spotted lungwort, purple-pink water avens (*Geum rivale*) which will keep flowering from spring through to autumn, pretty pink wood sorrel for summer and the spreading woodruff (*Galium odoratum*) which was once used to strew the floors of cottages and baronial halls for the deodorizing effect of its natural fresh scent.

If establishing a woodland area from scratch, you will probably have to introduce more shade-tolerant species gradually as the leaf canopy develops. For areas of broken shade along the woodland edges, or where deeper shade has yet to establish itself there are pretty foliaged alchemillas, stunning astilbes, tall foxgloves, iris, hostas and many hundreds more. There are even shade-tolerant grasses if you are seeking the effect of flowers among the grass: *Holcus lanatus* should grow well from broadcast seed.

Most wild plants can be sown directly on to the soil in early spring but will not flower until the following year. Planting selected species already established in pots will produce a much quicker effect and will flower the following season in smaller areas, and it is only expense and effort that prevents you hand-planting a much larger area with pot-grown plants. Alternatively, some vigorous creepers can be propagated simply by pressing a length of stem showing some root growth on to a patch of soil: ivy, the wild strawberry and periwinkles should all produce quick and attractive ground cover using this very simple technique.

60

Fig 62 *Roots, stems and foliage all contribute to the appeal of the shade or woodland garden.*

CREATING A WOODLAND AREA

As with any wildflower area, the ground has to be well prepared before you consider planting; lack of patience at this stage will only cause problems, a great deal of extra work and risk of failure later. Prepare the ground by digging over, carefully removing all perennial weeds. Try to finish preparing the ground ready for planting during the trees' dormant months when they will have a better chance of survival from the shock of upheaval. You should buy young bare-rooted native trees if you can. These seem to get away quicker than larger or container-grown plants. The larger trees may be useful for creating an instantly mature effect but the smaller whips are almost guaranteed to overtake them after around five years.

Autumn is the best time to plant your trees,

while the soil is still warm, encouraging the roots to establish themselves. Later in the year, winter planting is possible but remember that you will not be able to work the soil while it is wet or frozen and that bare-rooted plants do not like being kept out of the soil for long. It is essential that you keep the tree roots damp while the tree is waiting to be planted; give it a good extra soaking just before. At this stage, gently spread out the root ball, taking care not to break off any of the smaller rootlets; taking the opportunity to assess its size. Dig a hole just slightly larger than the root ball and deep enough so that it will rest at the same level in the ground as before; you will be able to see up the trunk or stem where the soil level was. Allow for a layer of well-rotted manure, compost or leaf-mould in the bottom of the hole — some tree planters like to turn over and drop in the square of turf cut from the top, grass-side down and cover with the precious top-soil. Back-fill, firming in well round the roots as you go, and give a thorough watering. Finish with a layer of mulch to help keep in the soil moisture and to keep down weeds. You may like to spread black plastic over the surface for about 18in (45cm) around the stem of the tree which will completely suppress any weeds for the first season. You can hide it under your regular mulch of bark chips or leaf-mould to disguise it.

Young trees should be staked if the site is exposed and protected with tree guards from rabbit and squirrel damage. If using a stake, it should be driven in firmly on the side of prevailing winds when preparing the hole; you will only require a short stake and a single tie as the tree must still be allowed flexible movement in the breeze. It is also important that you use a correct tie, one that is recommended for this use and not a piece of string or twine which will be too tight and retard or distort the growth of the trunk, maybe even kill the tree.

During the first year, newly planted trees and shrubs will require careful watering during dry spells. There will be a lot of plants competing for nutrients and moisture if you have planned your woodland area in a single stage. You may find it

Fig 63 The wonderfully dramatic feathery foliage of ferns will transform a damp shady corner into a stunning focal point, especially if you choose the majestic form of the royal fern, Osmunda regalis.

necessary to rig up some kind of automatic watering system to ensure your plants' survival.

COPPICING

Coppicing is an ancient woodland technique which involves cutting down certain trees almost to ground level at ten- to fifteen-year intervals. it means many larger species of trees can be usefully grown in smaller gardens by cutting them down every few years to keep them at a manageable size. It also allows more light to reach the flowering plants below. Coppiced trees such as willow and dogwood are useful for the woodland edge area where their whippy stems and fresh foliage look very attractive.

CHAPTER 6

The Natural Hedgerow

A well-planned and maintained hedgerow is a wonderful place to find all kinds of wildlife, providing the ideal habitat for song birds, insects and small mammals. With native woodland fast disappearing, it is the major existing habitats for semi-shade-loving species and is extremely valuable ecologically as a nesting site and source of food for birds and butterflies. From a more selfish point of view, it is also capable of providing year-round interest, making this an excellent-value wild-garden feature for any size of plot. A mixed hedge may include a wide range of shrubs, trees, climbers and wild flowers in a relatively small area; the fresh greenness of hawthorn and cherry plum and the heart-lifting creamy clusters of primrose flowers in spring; feathery chervil, cow parsley and hogweed in summer; the bright red hips of dog rose or sweet briar, the red and

Fig 64   The wild dog rose (Rosa canina) *has fine glossy leaves and delicious pink-white blooms. It makes an attractive element of a mixed hedgerow or a superb single-species hedge.*

Fig 65   *You should be aiming at a controlled tangle of hedgerow shrubs and climbers to provide an interesting display of leaves, flowers, fruits and berries through the seasons.*

bronze foliage of the field maple and the papery green cones of the wild hop in autumn.

A hedgerow makes an excellent boundary for a wild or semi-formal garden or good screening around a smaller wildflower feature. You should be aiming at around seventy per cent regularly spaced hawthorn plants – or quickthorn as it sometimes appropriately called as it grows and thickens fast and is ideal hedging material – plus a selection of other shrubs or trees planted in random groups along its length. Try to aim for a good variety of species to provide interest at different times of the year. This might be spiny blackthorn with its blue-black sloe berries; evergreen holly with bright berries so attractive to birds; or the rambling dog rose which produces a breath-taking display of single pink blooms in summer. The position of your hedge may influence your choice of shrubs, trees and wild flowers, and, of course, where it forms a garden boundary you will only enjoy the benefit of one side of it. A hedge running east to west will give you either an extremely sunny or very shady side; the ideal is a hedge which runs south-east/north-west with your garden on the north-east side so that it enjoys shade from the afternoon sun.

PLANTING A MIXED HEDGE

You should begin by preparing the ground by digging over and removing any perennial weeds before digging a trench about lft (30cm) wide.

Fork plenty of well-rotted manure, compost, peat or leaf-mould into the bottom to give your trees and shrubs a good start. As recommended when buying trees and shrubs for creating a woodland (*see* page 52), young bare-rooted native specimens are best and will grow more quickly. These should be bought and planted during autumn or winter when plants will be dormant. Autumn is the best time to plant as the soil will still be warm and this will encourage root growth. As is so often the case, you should keep roots damp and water well before planting.

Shrubs and trees should be planted in two staggered rows about 6–8in (15–20cm) apart, with around 1ft (30cm) between the plants to produce a good thick hedge. Planting shrubs at a 45-degree angle to the ground will encourage the

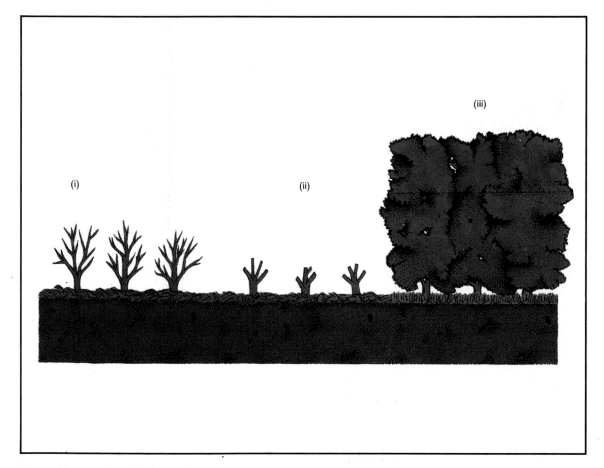

Fig 66 *How to plant a hedgerow*
(i) Two-year-old plants are put into your prepared trench around 20in(50cm) apart and the roots well mulched to keep in the moisture.
(ii) Cutting back hard with secateurs in the first spring will encourage bushy growth at the base. However, most evergreen species are best left for a couple of years to establish themselves.
(iii) The hedge will be ready for clipping roughly into shape after four to five years. You will be aiming at a slightly shaggy, dense tapered effect rather than a close-clipped look.

new shoots to grow vertically and produce a good thick base to the hedge. Alternatively, shrubs and trees could be pruned back to 6–8in (15–20cm) once they are planted to encourage bushy growth and good root development. Should the hedge look a little too thin for your liking once it is underway, you could always introduce some extra shrubs providing you remember they will need feeding as they will be competing with existing plants for nutrients. Place the plants in the trench, making sure the soil is at the same level as indicated on the stem and spreading the roots out gently. Back-fill with soil or manure, firm down well and water in thoroughly. Mulching around the roots with grass clippings, chopped bark, black polythene or even old carpet (covered with bark chips if you want an instant natural look) will help preserve water around the roots.

The hedge will need cutting back hard for the first two seasons to encourage dense growth. After that, trim it once a year until it reaches the height and thickness required. Trees are normally cut right back to achieve shrub status, but where

Fig 67 Providing it has a well-drained soil, holly (Ilex aquifolium) tolerates a wide range of conditions and makes an excellent, if prickly, hedge shrub with glossy green leaves, small white flowers and brilliant red berries irresistible to birds in winter.

Fig 68 Hawthorn (Crataegus monogyna) is a fast-growing shrub or tree with musky-scented blossoms in spring, red berries in autumn and attractive green leaves. It usually makes up the bulk of a wild hedgrow.

you have the space or want to add a little height and extra interest, selected specimens can be allowed to grow above the designated hedgeline, increasing the decorative and wild-food benefits of fruit, nuts and nectar. Keep them bushy by regular cutting; an oak is worth considering for the wide range of wildlife it supports but it will have to be coppiced (*see* page 62). A wayfaring tree, sometimes called spindle, is a wise choice as it has good autumn colour and pink seed pods.

An annual prune in early winter is best once the hedge is established to avoid disturbing birds' nests or spoiling nuts and berries in autumn or wasting buds and new leaf growth in spring. You should aim at a kind of tapered wedge shape, thicker at the bottom than the top to prevent snow resting heavy on the top and causing damage. Once established, you will notice a natural succession of wild flowers and wildlife such as birds, hedgehogs, voles and shrews.

If you are impatient or are hoping to see particular species of plants beneath your hedge, you can plant them yourself: lovely yellow archangel, the frequently seen herb Robert, hedge bedstraw, primrose, campion, bugle and a wide range of other traditional hedgerow flowers that will maintain interest from spring through to autumn. Most prefer a shady, damp and fertile soil, although many will tolerate any soil conditions. Some, like bloody crane's-bill, with its tiny mauve flowers and trailing stems of starburst foliage, and various of the St John's worts prefer a dry stony soil. Wild flowers can be raised from seed and transplanted when large enough to handle or be bought as small plants. Grass should appear spontaneously, but you could introduce a flower and grass mixture recommended for shady sites.

The area should need scything only once a year, and late winter is the best time before your spring bulbs begin to show. Flowering climbers such as honeysuckle (*Lonicera periclymenum*), old man's beard (*Clematis vitalba*) and wild hop (*Humulus lupulus*) will add body and interest to your hedge, but do not introduce them until your main shrubs and trees are well established so that they are not choked out.

CREATING A SINGLE-SPECIES HEDGE

Ideally, an established wildlife hedge should be allowed to grow slightly out of control so that trees and shrubs can flower and fruit freely, but this is not always practical in a restricted space and not ideal for nest-building anyway. If you are a bird-lover and particularly keen on creating a hedge that will make an ideal nesting place and source of food, you may like to create a single-species hedge. This might also suit your design plans for your garden better.

Fig 69 The wild hop (Humulus lupulus) *is a vigorous and attractive climber producing unusual lime-green, papery cone-like flowers that can look charming scrambling through a wild hedge.*

Fig 70 *The dog rose not only has lovely blooms and foliage, it also produces handsome hips in autumn to attract the birds.*

Fig 71 Gaps can be filled in existing hedgerows providing you feed the new seedling well as it will be competing with greedy mature shrubs.

Fig 72 An excellent ornamental shrub for hedgerows, the wayfaring tree (Viburnum lantana) makes a mass of creamy flowers in early summer and a show of red and black berries in autumn among a dense display of fine foliage.

If you are hoping to create an informal hedge to border a wild or semi-wild feature, you could plant sweet briar which will not only please the thrushes and blackbirds with its edible hips, but also the gardener by producing a mass of sweet-scented pink flowers. It needs to grow to a height of around 5ft (1.5m) and be at least 2ft (60cm) thick for nesting. Barberry (Pyracantha rogersiana) is an attractive evergreen which will grow to a width of 6ft (1.8m). It can be well clipped to a height of 5ft (1.5m) for nesting: the autumn berries are attractive to a wide range of birds and the spring flowers a great attraction to bees. Individual plants should be put in about 1½ft (50cm) apart and should have reached mature hedge status after around six years. Yew is a useful evergreen hedge which does not grow very fast so will only need clipping once a year. The birds enjoy its shelter and eat the red berries. Beech and hornbeam are also useful for clipping and thus make good semi-formal single-species hedges.

CHAPTER 7

Ponds and Marshes

A pond is one of the easiest and most satisfying wildlife features you can incorporate in your garden. Wonderfully adaptable, it can be as large as a lake or as small as a barrel on the patio, yet support a fascinating range of water plants. Apart from the pleasure of planning and observing what are often exotic-looking wild flowers, there is the enjoyment of simply watching reflections in the water or noting an extraordinary range of wildlife, from fish and insects to birds and small mammals. Even the smallest pond is extremely valuable environmentally, too, with so much of our wetlands disappearing each year. A natural water feature also looks extremely good when

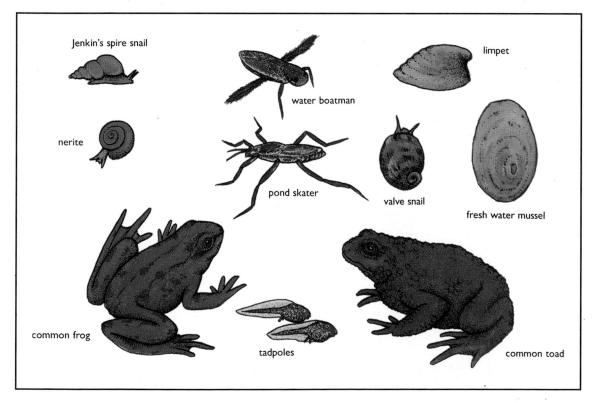

Fig 73 Any kind of water feature acts like an instant magnet to a wide range of wildlife, from snails and water beetles to larger frogs and toads. A bucket of mud from the bottom of an existing pond will provide a large number of species; or you can wait for them to appear spontaneously.

Fig 75   The smallest circular waterproof tub or container could be sunk in a corner of the garden or patio and surrounded with a dense arrangement of water-loving plants such as ferns and sedges to create a wonderfully intimate wild atmosphere.

designed in conjunction with other wildflower features, such as an area of meadowland, or sited close to a woodland area (but not so close that the water fills with leaves at the end of the year).

It is important to consider the exact position of your pond (or marsh) feature so that it looks as natural as possible and provides the best possible environment for plants and animals. An open site is best, away from any trees that will pollute the water with their leaves: in particular, avoid trees to the south and west as they will cast unwelcome shade — the majority of water-loving wild flowers prefer a sunny situation — and

Fig 74 (Opposite)   The well-planned wildflower pond can look superb in either a wild or more formal large garden, its dramatic blend of aquatic and pond-edge plants making an excellent focal point.

prevailing winds will be more likely to blow leaves into the water where they sink to the bottom, rot and cause it to go stagnant. A pond looks most in keeping in a natural hollow; if you are lucky enough to have a natural stream in the garden, use it to feed your pond and link the feature to other areas.

MAKING A POND

Small Containers

The simplest and smallest type of natural pond involves filling a suitable waterproof container with water and standing it in the garden or on the patio. Half barrels and old sinks are the most popular miniature features and, with around 3–4in (6–10cm) of soil or sand and gravel in the

71

Fig 76 Brandy bottle (Nuphar lutea) is an attractive yellow-flowered water-lily for large ponds, producing a mass of green leathery leaves and simple but bright yellow flowers.

base, can be successfully planted with smaller but no less beautiful water-plant species, and even stocked with a couple of fish. This type of raised pond feature has several other advantages despite its modest size. Re-using old containers looks far more natural than, say, a built-in raised pool covered in brick or stone. The advantage of height adds another dimension to a corner of the garden or looks just right when incorporated with an arrangement of plant pots and containers on a paved area; it is also easier to observe as it is nearer the eye, and thus ideal for handicapped garden users.

Sunken Ponds

More ambitious and capable of being built to virtually any size, a sunken pond is well worth the upheaval to install: for, providing it is correctly constructed and stocked, it is extremely easy to maintain in return for the hours of pleasure it offers. Initially, the shape must be as natural as possible: an irregular oval without too many elaborate inlets and curves and with gently shelved sides to create plenty of shallow water for wildlife. The central deep-water area should be at least 3ft (90cm) to ensure that pond inhabitants can survive the winter even if the surface freezes over. A large area of shallows is important for planting marginal species (those plants that like their roots submerged) and also makes it easier for small animals to get in and out of the water. Sloping sides are particularly important for concrete-lined pools as any ice forming on the sides should the pond freeze, will slide up rather than exert unsustainable pressure on the sides. A gentle slope means an incline of no more than 1:3 or soil will slip downwards.

The pond can be any size but it is a good idea to plan as big a feature as possible for a greater range of wildlife and easier-to-maintain ecological balance. Around 13–16sq. ft (4–5sq. m) is a good size, with a minimum depth of around 2½ft (75cm) at any point. Anything but the smallest pond should be dug out using a mechanical digger, and these can be hired by the day or weekend. Many are quite small and manageable but it is a good idea to check whether you have adequate access to the site and that other established features will not be at risk from accidental damage. Closer details, such as the angle of the sides, can easily be finished off with a garden spade.

You should begin by peeling back the turf in strips and rolling it turf-side inwards to be used elsewhere; water it regularly if you are not re-laying it immediately. Take off the topsoil carefully and store it separately; it will come in useful later either for planting marginal plants or other species requiring a good fertile compost. The

72

Fig 77   Planned and constructed as a single feature, a bog garden makes
a fine border to a natural pond and will extend the scope of plants you
can include to a fascinating range of marsh and bog species.

bulk of subsoil is excellent for creating a wildflower bank or similar landscaped feature in the garden.

When the rough shape of the pond is dug; finish by hand using a spirit-level to get it completely level and remove any stones or other sharp objects. Early spring is a good time for pond building as it will give plenty of time for construction to be completed, for the water to warm up and for plants to be given plenty of time to establish themselves before the end of the summer when they begin to die back.

METHODS OF LINING A POND

Clay Puddling

There are various ways a pond can be lined to make it waterproof. The most natural method and the one which simulates conditions in the wild is to clay puddle the base and sides. This system is a particularly good one to choose if your soil has a naturally high clay content, which makes it easier to work and less likely to crack or dry out. Not only does it look good, but clay puddling also provides ideal conditions for growing your favoured wildflower plants. If *in situ* subsoil is not suitable, you can buy a form of clay recommended for clay puddling ponds called Bentonite, but this can be expensive for anything but the smallest pools. The clay compound or clay soil should be well watered to make it sticky, then puddled or 'paddled' using your hands and feet (skilled operators can use mechanical diggers in large ponds) until a continuous sticky layer has been created. It is hard work and not easy to get right on first attempt. The clay is finished with a layer of soil for plants to be established.

Concrete

Where clay puddling is not practical or desirable, ponds can be lined with concrete (in the past, this was the only alternative). If correctly mixed and applied, this has the advantage of being strong and durable, capable of lasting for years and allowing you (and animals) to stand in the pond without risk of damage. The big drawback of concrete is that unless you are experienced at handling it, it can be tricky to apply successfully into the necessary bowl shape of a pond; also, if incorrectly mixed and the right additives not incorporated, it may be at risk from frost damage which means draining the pool to make awkward repairs. There is also an aesthetic problem in that concrete is not always compatible with the concept of the pond as a natural, wild-plant feature.

Fig 78 The sword-shaped leaves and bright fruits of the 'Gladdon' or stinking iris (Iris foetidissima) are an unusual and handsome sight which will do well in fertile but well-drained soil. This is a useful plant that will tolerate sun or shade.

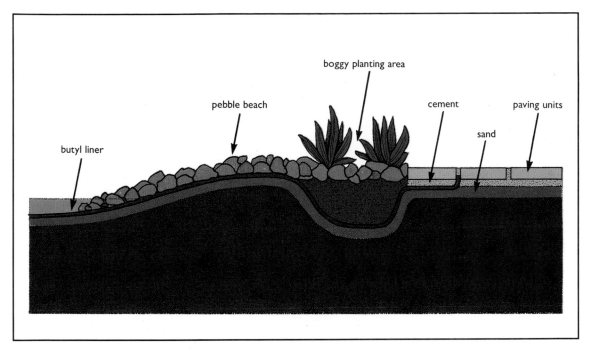

Fig 79 A pebble beach is an attractive and very natural-looking way to disguise the edges of a plastic- or rubber-lined pond. For the best effect, the pebbles should be run right into the shallows which will also encourage birds and small mammals to use the water.

If you do decide it is the best option, your excavation will have to be shuttered with timbers before the concrete is applied. Ready-mixed concrete is to be strongly recommended for medium to large ponds as it must be applied swiftly and evenly. Again, check that you have access and adequate space to put it. A concrete-lined pond cannot be used immediately; you must fill it with water and drain a couple of times over a period of three to four weeks to remove the poisonous lime content.

Flexible Liners

The modern and convenient way to line ponds and pools is to use a stout flexible liner which moulds itself naturally and easily to whatever size and shape you have excavated. Polythene and PVC are the cheapest types but do not last more than a few years. It is better to pay a little more

Fig 80 Reeds and grasses can contribute an interesting range of foliage shapes and colours in the rich soil surrounding a pond or marsh. Wood millet (Milium effusum aurea) makes a glorious clump of golden fluttering pennants.

75

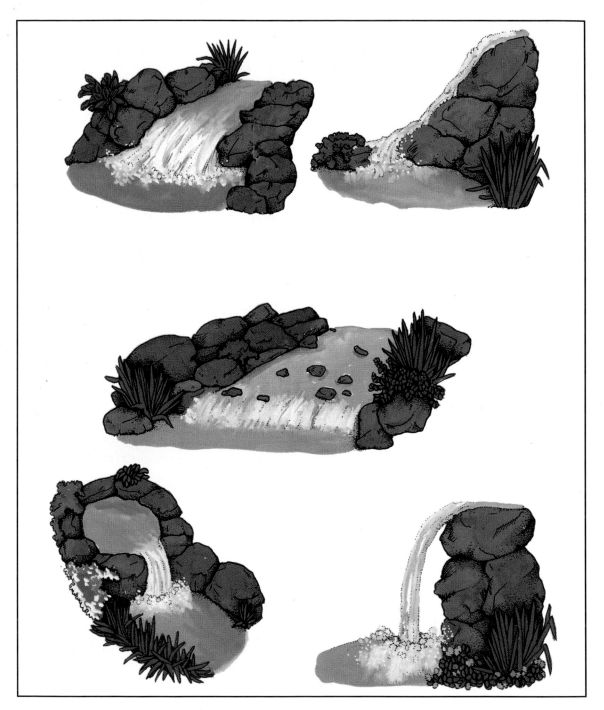

Fig 81 A waterfall is an excellent way to link a wild pond to a rocky wildflower feature. Achieving an authentic effect can take time: it helps to study waterfall formations in the wild to get it right.

for tough butyl liner, which should last for decades and generally comes in unobtrusive black, although blue and other colours may be available.

You must first estimate exactly how much liner you need, allowing for a generous amount to be tucked over the sides and hidden under your chosen edging material. The material stretches, so no other surplus is required in your estimations – try to calculate as closely as possible as the material is expensive.

You will need to make your excavation about 8in (20cm) deeper to allow for lining material beneath the rubber or plastic sheeting. When you are sure the pond area is level and that there are no sharp stones, spread over a 'blinding' layer of sand to a depth of about 2in (5cm). Special polypropylene matting over the top of this is intended to protect the liner from tears and rips but, if you cannot afford this, old newspapers or carpet make an acceptable substitute. The liner is laid loosely into the hole and secured along the edges with smooth boulders; do not use anything sharp that might damage the material. Take care not to pull the liner tight, crease it or damage it with your boots or shoes. Lay a second protective layer of matting or newspaper over the liner, and top with around 5–6in (12–15cm) of topsoil.

The pond can now be filled by resting a hose-pipe on a piece of matting in the bottom and allowing the water to trickle in slowly without disturbing the soil and exposing the liner. The weight of the water will gradually pull the liner tight against the sides, but do keep an occasional eye on it as it fills to ensure that there are no awkward creases or rucks. Do not put in any plants or livestock for a couple of days if using tap water, to allow the chlorine to evaporate.

DISGUISING THE EDGES

Whatever liner method you choose, careful thought will have to be given to disguising the edges of the pond to create the most natural

Fig 82 Creeping Jenny (Lysimachia nummularia) *is one of the best ground-cover plants for damp fertile soil. It makes a dense carpet of bright-green shiny leaves and a mass of yellow flowers.*

effect. Observing water features in the wild will give you some idea of how it should look, and if you have managed to landscape your pond with other garden features you will already have a head start. A rocky feature coming down to the water's surface could be extended around the edges of the water to hide the liner and provide plenty of crevices for frogs, toads and other small animals. A flat-topped rock protruding slightly above the water's surface will also be appreciated by those creatures that enjoy basking in the sun.

77

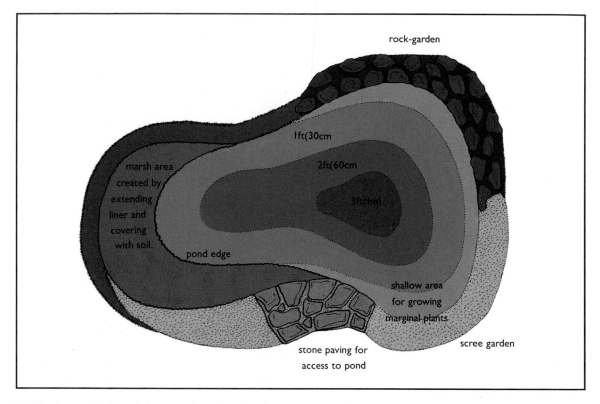

rock-garden

1ft(30cm

2ft(60cm

marsh area
created by
extending
liner and
covering
with soil.

3ft(1m)

pond edge

shallow area
for growing
marginal plants

scree garden

stone paving for
access to pond

*Fig 83   A natural informal shape can be planned to incorporate a variety
of wetland habitats for your plants, from marsh and marginal planting
areas to rocky outcrops and pebble beaches.*

Paving is very practical for providing a firm footing and somewhere dry to sit and observe pond wildlife, but it does not always look particularly natural. It really does depend on how wild you want the feature to look and how it fits the rest of your garden scheme. The best way to tackle it is to leave plenty of gaps between brick, stone or concrete slabs and to fill them with soil and sand to encourage grasses and wild flowers to establish themselves and soften the harder outlines of the paving.

One of the most natural effects is achieved where the pond forms part of, or is close to, a lawn or meadow: the grass can be extended using turfs, right to the water's edge, to merge with lush marginal planting.

Another very natural-looking way to tackle the pond edges and one which extends the scope of wild flowers you can incorporate into your garden, is to extend a flexible liner under the soil to create a marsh. Obviously, this would not be practical all around the pond as you would have no access to the water, but on one or two sides and combined with another edging treatment, it looks remarkably effective and may help the pond to merge gradually into the rest of the garden. Ideally, your marsh should be positioned so that it takes the natural overspill from the pond to keep the soil saturated; you will have to do the job in hot dry weather using a hose-pipe. If you like to watch birds, you might like to consider installing a small shingle beach on at least one of the approaches to the water. Shingle or sand and gravel should be gently sloped into the water, encouraging birds and small animals to go right down to the water to drink or bathe.

PLANTING UP THE POND

Water and marginal plants are normally bought from specialist nurseries or acquired from friends with already established wildflower ponds: because they tend to be rampant growers you do not need a large number of specimens to provide a well-covered and mature effect within a single season. When planning a wildflower pond, the problem can be getting hold of native plants rather than exotic hybrid varieties. Plants can be grown from seed but they are difficult to germinate. If your pond is large and you need a great number of plants, you are better off relieving friends and family of clumps and cuttings when cleaning out their ponds; or propagating from your own plant stocks. Never be tempted to raid ponds in the wild.

Plants are categorized quite clearly as: those that rest on the bottom of the pond; those that float freely on the surface; plants which grow with their roots in the marginal shallows and pond edge; and marsh plants that simply like the proximity of water and a damp soil. As a general guide, you should avoid tall or rampant species if the pond is rather small. Even with larger areas of water, the taller species should be grown to the north side of the pond to prevent them casting shade over the pond. Trees close to the water's edge are usually avoided for the same reason: shade creates algae problems on the water's surface and inhibits the growth of many flowering plants. Because the majority of water plants are vigorous growers, it is worth growing underwater and marginal varieties in special open baskets rather than directly in the water-submerged soil. In a small or medium-sized pond, baskets will help keep plants under control; in a larger pool they are still useful for lifting and thinning or splitting the plants when they have grown rather large.

You will need a range of oxygenating plants; these replace lost oxygen in the water and are important for keeping the pond healthy. Good oxygenators include the common Canadian pondweed (*Elodea canadensis*) which tends to get a bit out of hand if not kept in regular check: water milfoil (*Myriophyllum*) which produces tiny

Fig 84   A natural pond should include a range of depths, from gently sloping shallows to a minimum depth of 2½ft(80cm) to prevent at least part of the pond freezing in winter. Marsh species grow in rich damp soil, marginal plants in the shallows, and aquatic plants in the deepest part of the pool.

Fig 85   Elegant and ideally suited to growing in the rich damp soil along
the edge of a pond or marsh, the summer snowflake (Leucojum
aestivum) is an easy-to-grow bulb in sun or shade, producing a clump of
spiky leaves and delicate white bells in spring.

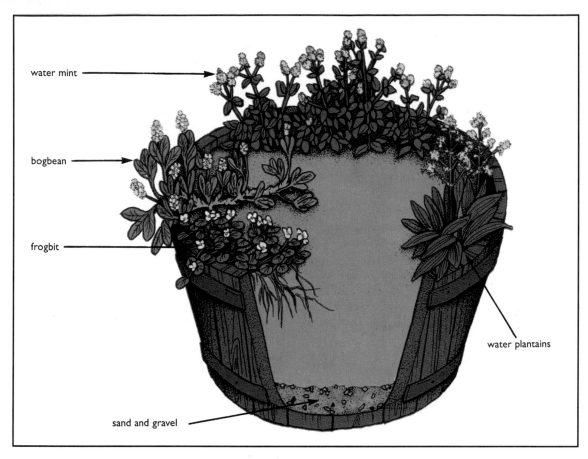

water mint

bogbean

frogbit

water plantains

sand and gravel

Fig 86 A miniature pond is a fascinating feature for the no-garden wild garden and is easily created using an old half barrel. Water plants should be chosen carefully so that they do not look out of scale and cut back regularly to prevent them choking the tub. Providing you include a couple of oxygenating water plants, such as water milfoil, and place a few stones or rocks in the bottom, even this tiny feature will attract a range of snails and insects.

white flowers; and, perhaps prettiest of all, the water violet (*Hottonia palustris*) which makes a dense mat of foliage in the water and has delicate, yellow-centred lilac flowers. You need approximately one small cutting of a suitable oxygenator plant per 1 sq. ft (30sq. cm) of water surface. They can be planted in containers or weighted with a pebble and anchored to the bottom of the deepest part of the pond.

There are other plants which prefer either to be semi-submerged or to float on the surface of the water. Arrowhead, (*Sagittaria sagittifolia*), with its striking leaves, and spiky sweet grass (*Glyceria maxima*) are only two which like to be rooted in deep water. Then there are the lovely water-lilies of course, without which no pond seems truly complete. These generally require a depth of water of at least 6in (15cm), although there are dwarf varieties, suitable for small and shallow ponds or pond containers, which require less water. Water-lilies are usually grown in containers standing bricks or blocks in the water so that the leaves and flowers just rest on the surface of the water. Most common are the white water-lily (*Nymphaea alba*) and the yellow brandy bottle (*Nuphar lutea*).

Around the water's edge, with their roots in the rich damp soil of the shallows, you will want to plant a selection of marginal or emergent plants. These include some of the most exciting and stunning wildflower and foliage effects, from the umbrella-like sweet galingale (*Cyperus longus*) and fragrant water mint (*Mentha aquatica*) to the long-lived spread of the blue-flowered water forget-me-not (*Myosotis scorpoides*) which blooms right through from spring to the autumn.

Other plants enjoy being close to the water's edge and thrive in the damp but not waterlogged soil of marsh or bog conditions. Here you can plant the stately flag iris with its lovely yellow blooms, tall purple loosestrife (*Lythrum salicaria*),

easy to grow but delicate bogbean (*Menyanthes trifoliata*) and the tall flowering rush (*Butomus umbellatus*). Vigorous spreading plants, such as the bright yellow marsh marigold (*Caltha palustris*) and cuckoo flower, will gradually spread out towards surrounding grass areas as they self-seed.

STOCKING THE POND

You will be surprised at the variety of small wildlife, such as amphibians, insects and even fish, that will appear quite spontaneously as soon as

*Fig 87 Water-loving plants can provide autumn interest, too: stinking iris (*Iris foetidissima*) not only has elegant sword-shaped leaves and fine yellow and purple flowers, but also produces glowing orange seeds.*

*Fig 88 Ferns usually do well in the rich damp soil of a pond edge and marsh. One of the most spectacular is the tall royal fern, (*Osmunda regalis*) which produces tall feathery clumps and turns a wonderful red-gold in autumn.*

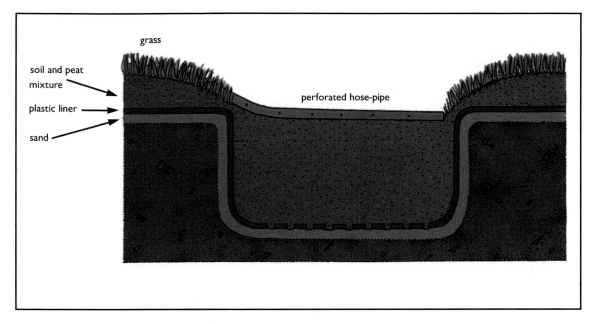

grass

soil and peat mixture

plastic liner

sand

perforated hose-pipe

Fig 89 If a pond is impractical, a marsh or wetland is easily and quickly created using a perforated plastic liner laid on a layer of sand or pebbles for good drainage. A trickling or punctured hose-pipe will keep the area suitably damp.

your pond is established, probably borne there as eggs on the beaks of birds. Even the smallest, town-bound pond will be enhanced by exotic-looking dragon-flies and the comical sight of frogs. A bucket of pond mud from a neighbouring pool will introduce hundreds more creatures; you will also find that the plants you use to stock your pond will introduce a certain number of small creatures, such as snails and insects. If you want to keep ornamental fish, you will have to build them a separate pool or they will gobble up all your tadpoles.

A MARSH OR BOG GARDEN

If a full-scale pond is not practical or suitable – if you have young children, for example – or if you would simply like to grow a few of the spectacular marsh and water's edge wild flowers, a marsh or bog garden is easy to install and maintain. A piece of punctured pool-lining material laid over a natural hollow or shallow excavation

no more than 15in (45cm) deep should be covered in a 3in (8cm) layer of pebbles for drainage and a good moist soil. You must keep the area damp; in dry weather a continuous trickle from a hose-pipe should be sufficient. It need not form part of the main pond but could be a separate feature in its own right; or be integrated with another wildflower feature such as an area of meadowland or rock. Plants should be chosen carefully: avoid the dramatic but incongruous hybrid forms readily available at specialist water centres.

If you have a large, natural area of poorly drained land at your disposal, you could easily put it to good use as a wildflower wetland meadow. Wetland meadow seed mixture is available and can be sown as soon as you have eliminated any perennial weeds. Plants you could expect to see in such an area might include the delicate bell-like flowers of water avens displayed against its large green leaves, the exotic fritillary; pretty ragged-robin (*Lychnis flos-cuculi*) and yellow loosestrife (*Lysimachia vulgaris*). Wetland

Fig 90 A small water pump could be used to create a small stream, almost hidden by waterside plants, to make a splendid complementary feature to a wildflower woodland or meadow.

meadows are designed to dry out on the surface over the summer months, sealing in the moisture underneath, and can by scythed in autumn. Like ponds, a marsh or bog garden can also be miniaturized into a wildflower tub or container for the patio or awkward corner of the garden (*see* page 71).

MAINTAINING THE POND

Once established, ponds need very little attention. The best time to consider a 'spring clean' is in autumn when plants and wildlife are beginning their dormant stage and will be least disturbed. A vital end-of-season job is to keep the water clear of leaves from nearby trees; if they are allowed to pollute the water, they will quickly make it stagnant. Plants will need

thinning, dividing or cutting back in autumn as they tend to be invasive and can easily take over. However, this is a relatively easy task – especially if water-submerged species have been planted in baskets as has been recommended. It is always a good idea to use unwanted plant material in exchange for new species with fellow pond owners.

Providing they are not allowed to get out of hand and cover the whole water's surface, submerged or floating oxygenating plants, such as water milfoil and frogbit, will help to maintain the correct ecological balance and prevent the build-up of ugly green algae. This may still be a problem in small ponds, especially if you have to use chlorinated tap water to top up after a spell of dry weather. In this case, it may be necessary to buy a small electric filter to keep the water healthy.

CHAPTER 8

Practical Matters

Wildflower gardening is rewarding and capable of being adapted to virtually any size and style of garden; but on a practical level, it must be approached from a slightly different standpoint from familiar, conventional gardening methods if you want to enjoy success. Wildflower seed is not as predictable as modern highly bred plant varieties; it may not germinate when and where you expect it to; plants tend to grow like mad under ideal conditions but not at all if soil and light requirements are not right.

WHERE TO GET YOUR PLANTS

Generally speaking, growing from seed is cheaper but time-consuming and may produce far more plants than you need. If you are only

Fig 91 Many shrubs and trees, such as the glossy holly, rely on the birds that eat their bright berries to spread and propagate the seeds, the coating cleverly broken down by the bird's digestive system.

looking for one or several plants, you are better off buying individual plants from a specialist nursery. Once established – and given the right conditions – these should flourish, and you can take cuttings or collect your own seedlings should you require further stock which are far quicker and more reliable methods of propagation.

Both plants and seeds can be bought from the specialist wildflower and herb nurseries; some will provide plants by post. Particularly useful, especially for larger areas, are the specially formulated grass- and flower-seed mixtures, usually recommended for a specific soil type. It is worth contacting your local wildlife trust organization. Plants, cuttings, runners and seeds should be available at certain times of the year with the advantage that they are fresher and that they will be locally collected so more likely to flourish in your own garden.

Collecting Your Own Seed

You can collect seed from the wild providing you do not touch any of the ninety two listed protected species as detailed on page 124. New species are added to the list all the time, so do check current legislation before you go hunting. Even bearing this in mind, amateur wildflower gardeners tend to be a little too enthusiastic – and dreadfully wasteful – when collecting seed. You should remember that a single bell-like bloom might supply as many as 100 seeds; there really is no point in ripping up the whole plant, roots and all, as it is simply wasted. The secret of success when collecting your own seed is to catch it at exactly the right time when it has ripened. As a rule, this is when the seed head has dried out and turned brown. If the seed inside is still green and moist when you go to collect it, leave it another few days or so, depending on the weather. Any plants, such as cat's ear, which produce dandelion-clock seed heads, are easy to collect but have to be harvested before they blow away. Some plants, for example cowslip and oxlip, make the job easy for you by displaying the seeds in upright containers; others, such as poppies, enclose the seed in a capsule which has to be tipped up to see if the seed is ripe and falls out readily.

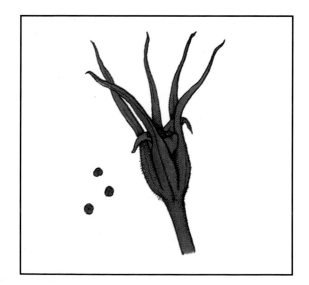

Fig 92   If not collected, capsule-forming wild flowers will eventually tip their seed out on to the ground below where the seedlings can be easily collected and used next year as required.

Fig 93   Some species, like dandelions, produce attractive fluffy seed heads designed to be dispersed by wind. You should pull off the individual 'parachute' seeds gently and store in a paper bag.

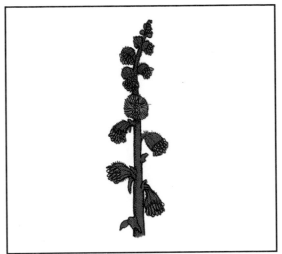

Fig 94   The most difficult seed to collect is the type that is designed to catapult itself a great distance by means of a trigger system, such as meadow crane's-bill. The best way to catch the seed when it is ripe is to tie a paper bag over the seed heads as soon as the flowers are over, or to cut off the seed heads before they are ripe and ripen them in a container covered with muslin to prevent the seeds escaping.

Fig 95   Different methods of seed dispersal among wild flowers are fascinating and ingenious: some, like agrimony, have hooked or prickly seed heads designed to attach themselves to the fur of passing animals.

A paper bag is the best device for collecting seeds; never a plastic one as it encourages moisture and fungal growth. There are some plants that must be harvested before they are ripe: these are usually species like members of the crane's-bill family which naturally broadcast their seed when it is ripe, making them imposs- ible to collect at the appropriate time. A paper bag tied over the seed heads as soon as flowering is finished is one way to attempt to catch some seed; another is to cut the heads when they are almost ripe but still a little green, and ripen them in a muslin-covered container in a sunny place. It is important to collect seed on a dry day or it will go mouldy.

To store your own seed – and you are sure to have more than you need – you can save par- ticular species for future years or for swapping with other wildflower enthusiasts in well-labelled, vacuum-sealed plastic boxes. Putting these into the refrigerator at a temperature of around 2°C (36°F) will help them to keep indefinitely. Silica packets in the containers will help to prevent seed getting damp and mouldy.

Exchanging cuttings with fellow wildflower en- thusiasts is a most useful and economical way to acquire plants; some, such as primroses and cowslips, can be successfully divided for quick and economical results.

GROWING FROM SEED

Because wild flowers are used to poor soil and stringent conditions, your chances of success are really quite good, as long as you have patience and a basic understanding of their particular re- quirements. Some plants are easier to propagate than others; meadow plants, for example, are relatively easy; marsh and woodland species are more difficult.

You can sow seed straight into the ground, in seed trays or, best of all, in raised seed-beds, preferably somewhere in the garden where you can virtually forget all about it until you see signs

Fig 96   Plants that produce bulbs can be increased by lifting and gently separating the little bulblets that form.

Fig 97   Woody perennial plants can be propagated from softwood cuttings taken during summer.

of life; unlike cultivated seeds, germination might take up to two years. A great many wild flowers start life on the rubbish tip where they have been thrown out under the assumption that they have come to nothing. Do not take this as a hard-and-fast rule, however; some wild flowers germinate extremely quickly – cornfield species like corn cockle and corn marigold will be flowering within a couple of months. Seed trays and beds do not need too rich a soil: after sowing, firm down the soil, water and net to protect from bird damage. Young plants may need protecting from slug damage.

Many make the mistake of sowing seed in spring. While this is acceptable, it is much better, especially for a beginner, to sow in autumn when seed would be naturally set in the wild. This is maybe the reason why some seeds take so long to germinate – they need that dormant spell of cold weather to prepare the seed case. You need only resort to artificial vernalization – that is, putting them in the freezer at two-day intervals, two days in and two days out – if you have missed a season and want to germinate your seeds quickly.

Sowing Directly into the Ground

The ground should be thoroughly prepared so that there is no risk of competitive weeds and ensuring that the soil is level and finely raked for efficient germination. Early spring or autumn is the best time to sow (see individual location chapters). If you are using a pre-prepared wild-flower mixture, you need approximately 1oz (4g) per square yard/metre for grass and flower mixtures; ½–¾oz (1–2g) per square yard/metre for flower seed. The best way to ensure even distribution is to divide up a large area into smaller plots, using stakes and string, and to divide the seed into a corresponding number of parts. Seed should be scattered or broadcast by clasping a small amount in your closed fist and swinging the hand from side to side as the seed slips through your fingers. If you are sowing flowers and grasses separately, the grasses should be broadcast first and then the flowers. It is important to sow grass seed evenly to achieve a balanced effect, but wild flowers actually look more effective if they grow in groups or drifts of a single species. After sowing, the area should be rolled to press the seed into the surface of the soil. There is no need to water. The same technique should be applied to sowing wildflower seed directly into beds and borders: prepare a fine tilth, eradicate any perennial weeds, broadcast the seed and roll or tread in, then leave them to let the seasons do their work.

Planting in Seed-Beds

Creating permanent seed-beds in a corner of the garden to make a kind of nursery area, saves seeds hanging about in pots where you might get impatient and want to move or be tempted to dispose of them, especially when growing biennials such as foxgloves and mullein. The area should be cleared thoroughly first of any perennial weeds, such as dock and nettle, using a garden fork. When you have produced a fine tilth, rake it and roll it (providing the weather and soil are reasonably dry). When sowing fine seed in trays or beds, mix it with sand so that you can see it in the drills. Cover lightly by raking the soil or drawing your finger over it, and net against birds.

Fig 99 Dandelions produce feathery parachute-like seeds which can be collected in a paper bag.

Fig 98 A root cutting is made by slicing off a thick section of root making sure it includes a bud.

Fig 100 Clump-forming herbaceous and water plants can be lifted and divided to keep them under control and create new plants in autumn.

89

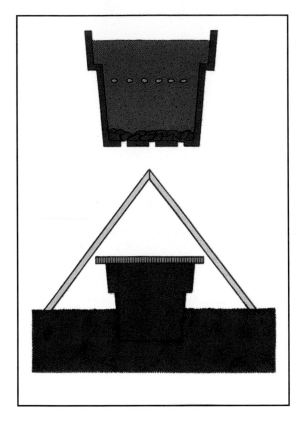

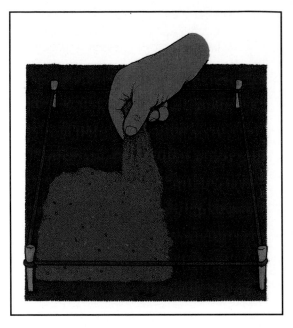

Fig 102   Even distribution of grass and wildflower seed mixtures is most easily achieved by dividing the plot into more easily managed sections and broadcasting the seed in the appropriate proportions.

Fig 101   Cloches protect wildflower seed from wind or rain but still allow frost to do its job. Plant directly into nursery beds or in pots, which should be half buried in the ground.

Planting in Trays

Prepare seed trays by filling them with a good gritty compost – not a peat-based compost as peat supplies are at risk from over-use by gardeners; you may like to experiment instead with one of the new peat substitutes such as coco-fibre. Plants which are difficult to germinate, such as marsh plants, may do better in trays; keeping the soil suitably moist. Water with a fine rose and cover with a sheet of glass or, better still, place under an open-ended cloche. This keeps the rain from washing all the seeds into a corner or the wind from blowing them away, yet still allows the frost in to do its necessary work. You can leave the trays uncovered and let the

seeds take their chance as they would in their natural habitat. Sown in the autumn, plants should germinate the following February; keep an eye on them. Keep the soil moist; standing the trays on damp soil or an old piece of carpet may help to keep the soil moist longer.

NEW PLANTING METHODS

You can buy shaped and moulded 'growing cells' which are expensive, but because they reduce root disturbance when planting on, they may be worth considering, especially for larger wildflower seed, such as meadow crane's-bill or cowslip which can be planted individually. When the young plants are large enough to handle, they are simply popped out using a pencil or special tool and potted on. If you water them first, they tend to come out more easily.

GROWING FROM CUTTINGS

Any wild plant that puts out runners, such as yellow archangel and bugle, is worth propagating from cuttings. This can be a particularly useful way to generate new plants from species such as meadow crane's-bill and violets whose seeds are naturally broadcast and which tend to shoot away as soon as ripened. Cut between each layer of leaves, or layer by pegging down. Some plants, such as lady's smock, can be grown from leaf cuttings – like begonias, they will root from leaves pressed on to the soil.

WILD GARDEN MAINTENANCE

Do not be misled into thinking that because you are aiming at a natural semi-wild effect, your garden or wildflower feature is able to look after itself.

Fig 104   A nursery bed in a corner of the garden means seeds can be left undisturbed until they germinate. Seedlings can later be lifted and transplanted into rows a few inches (five centimetres) apart until ready for planting out.

Fig 103   Plants with capsule-like seed heads such as poppies will readily shed their seed when ripe if you tip them up and shake them into a paper bag.

Fig 105   Plants with branching seed heads can be snipped off when fully dried and ripe, and the seed rubbed off between your fingers.

Fig 107 *As stunning as any cultivated hybrid, meadow crane's-bill* (Geranium pratense) *deserves pride of place in the wildflower border, where it will quickly spread to form a dense clump of attractive foliage and bright flowers.*

Fig 108 *Honesty* (Lunaria annua) *contains its ripe seeds in handy transparent pouches.*

Maintenance need not be a burden; but a regular annual routine will ensure it does not get out of hand and start to look not wild and informal, but an unsightly tangled mess; nor will you want to allow particularly invasive weeds to take over. Other routine garden tasks are mainly unnecessary.

There is no need to feed a wildflower area as too rich a soil will not suit them. If the soil is extremely sandy, chalky or clay-bound you could beneficially introduce a little organic matter in the form of organic compost or spent mushroom compost to improve its texture.

You should be saved any problems with pests,

Fig 106 (Opposite) The wildflower meadow needs mowing after the flowers are finished and have set seed for next year. The hay should be allowed to dry before raking and removing to prevent it mulching down.

too: since wild plants naturally attract a wide range of predatory and other insects, a natural balance should be attained. This may not work in practice where the wild feature is extremely small or located in towns or cities. Here you should try to keep plants as healthy as possible and are recommended to avoid chemical feeds which not only produce too much foliage growth, but also seem to invite aphid attack. Much better, if plants are in tubs, containers or a limited space, is to feed with a liquid seaweed compound. There are two natural pesticides, pyrethrum and derris, that will deal with most pests and problems but which should only be applied in the evening as they can be harmful to bees, ladybirds and fish.

Weeding is another garden chore that takes on a whole new meaning in the wildflower garden. You will want to leave self-seeded flowering

93

Fig 109   A wildflower bank could be created using the soil excavated from another garden feature such as a pond. Alternatively, build it up using woody garden compost material such as pruned branches, cuttings, grass mowings and dead leaves. Given time to rot down, this creates a good mound for plants preferring a humus-rich soil.

Fig 110   A mulch of leaf-mould or chopped bark will get woodland wild flowers off to the right start before the trees become established and do the job quite naturally themselves.

species from year to year, although these may require some modicum of control. Selective weeding will be necessary if one particularly vigorous species is not to dominate, or an unwanted plant intrude. You will soon learn to recognize which plantlets you want to keep and which need pulling; buy a good weed identification book if you are doubtful. You will find many 'weeds' are quite decorative and the philosophy of: 'well it looks pretty and it is filling a space so I'll leave it' is quite a good one to adopt in the wild garden with annual species.

Perennials, particularly those that spread by means of creeping roots, such as couch grass and buttercup, are a different matter and once established can be extremely difficult to eradicate. Try to remove from the soil as many tiny pieces of root as you can find as these will grow vigorously to make new unwelcome plants. Weeds are not normally a problem in grass and

Fig III Bulbs and corms will divide and multiply automatically from year to year; cyclamen will do best in bare soil – new plants and corms are available from specialist nurseries.

Fig 112 Vigorous climbing plants can often be propagated from cuttings, like the wild hop, Humulus lupulus.

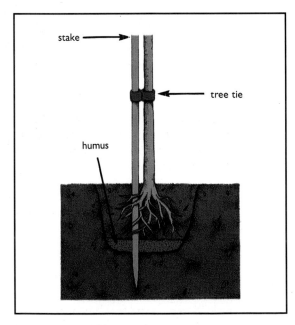

Fig 113 In exposed conditions, saplings should be supported by a short stake well stabilized in the planting hole.

meadowland areas where cutting and natural competition tend to keep things under control.

Flowering meadows will need regular mowing (see page 36) to maintain an attractive variety of flowers; left uncut, they will revert to mainly grass with a few of the more persistent wild flowers. Woodland gardens require equally minimum maintenance: fallen leaves should be left to rot down and create valuable leaf-mould to feed woodland wild flowers. Fallen branches and rotting logs are also worth leaving as a useful habitat for all kinds of insects and fungi. You will find that many flowers self-seed quite readily on the woodland floor if this balance is maintained; alternatively, you could sow individual species or a woodland mixture the first spring or autumn after planting your saplings. It is best not to underplant with bulbs and pot-grown plants until the young trees reach a height of at least 5ft (1.5m) tall.

Hedgerows require annual attention, for once they grow too thick or too tall they can be virtually impossible to bring back under control.

Fig II4 The bright fruits of the hawthorn, Crataegus monogyna.

They do not need to be closely and formally clipped but trimming will be necessary, as described on page 66. When trimming, look out for any self-seeded saplings that need removing before they grow too large, and also any unwanted suckers.

CALENDAR OF WILDFLOWER CARE

Spring Sow seed for next year and plant pot-grown specimens to flower this summer. Weed out any seedlings you do not want in wildflower beds and borders. Mow late-summer-flowering meadows if necessary.

Summer Flowering lawns and spring and early-summer-flowering meadows will need cutting. Keep an eye on marsh and pond areas during dry spells and top up with water where necessary.

Autumn Now is the ideal time to sow seed for next year, including annual meadow and cornfield mixtures, and to plant trees, shrubs and bulbs. Late-summer-flowering meadows will need cutting now. Thin invasive water plants and clean out the pond if it has silted up.

Winter Planting can continue while the garden is not frozen or too waterlogged. Prune the hedgerow and cut back to shape young trees as necessary.

97

CHAPTER 9

List of Plants

Check which types of plant grow locally as a guide to what will flourish in your area, and obtain your seeds and plants locally wherever possible. If you live in an area which suffers from particularly low temperatures, choose only the hardier species.

CODE

P   Perennial
A   Annual
B   Biennial

Agrimony   ('Church Steeples')
Agrimonia eupatoria (P)
Height: 6in–2ft/60cm.
Season: Summer.
Environment: Sunny border; meadow.
Slender spikes of pale yellow, star-shaped flowers are held above finely cut leaves. The plant has a pleasant fruity scent attractive to bees and insects and large hairy seeds in autumn.

Amphibious Bistort   *Polygonum amphibium* (P)
Height: 20in/50cm (land) 3ft/lm (water).
Season: Summer.
Environment: Marsh and pond.
A tall water's edge plant with long-stalked leaves. The flowers are pinkish spires.

Arrowhead   *Sagittaria sagittifolia* (P)
Height: 1–3ft/30–90cm.
Season: Summer.
Environment: Marsh and pond.
Ornamental, arrow-shaped leaves rise up out of the water. Attractive white flowers splashed with purple grow in small clusters on the flowering stems.

Autumn Hawkbit   *Leontodon autumnalis* (P)
Height: 6–20in/15–50cm.
Season: Summer, autumn.
Environment: Sunny border; meadow.
Dandelion-like yellow flowers and long, toothed leaves grow from the base of the stem.

Basil Thyme   *Acinos arvensis* (A)
Height: 4–8in/10–20cm.
Season: Summer, early autumn.
Environment: Sunny border; wall.
With small fragrant leaves and bright violet two-lipped flowers with white blotches on lower lip, this creeping, sprawling herbal plant is useful for planting in the crevices of walls and in between paving.

Biting Stonecrop   *Sedum acre* (P)
Height: 1–4in/2–10cm.
Season: Summer.
Environment: Sunny border; wall.
A fast-spreading plant with golden-yellow, tiny star-shaped flowers. Its many spreading branches are covered with fleshy, stubby leaves. Some consider this plant invasive.

Black Medick   *Medicago lupulina* (P)
Height: 2–20in/5–50cm.
Season: Summer.
Environment: Sunny border; meadow.
Low-growing plant with small heads of clear yellow flowers. The tiny rounded leaflets are covered in fine downy hair. Distinctive kidney-shaped seeds go black when ripe.

Blackthorn *Prunus spinosa* (P)
Height: 12ft/4m.
Season: Spring.
Environment: Sunny border; meadow; woodland; hedgerow.
With white blossom in spring and dark sloe berries in summer and early autumn, this is a good-value hedgerow plant.

Bladder Campion *Silene vulgaris* (P)
Height: 10in–3ft/25–90cm.
Season: Late spring, summer.
Environment: Sunny border; meadow.
Small white flowers grow from inflated bladder-like calyces. The plant produces a pleasant clove-

Fig 115 The Burnet rose (Rosa pimpinellifolia) is a low-growing shrub with beautifully scented flowers.

like aroma at night. Waxy, greyish-green foliage tastes like green peas.

Bramble *Rubus fruticosus* (P)
Height: 3ft/90cm.
Season: Summer, autumn.
Environment: Hedgerow; meadow.
Quickly spreading roots make this a shrub that must be kept in check. Flowers vary from white to cerise. Clusters of blackberries appear from August onwards.

Broom *Sarrothamnus scoparius* syn.
(*Cytisus scoparius*) (P)
Height: 8ft/2.5m.
Season: Summer.
Environment: Sunny border.
Deciduous shrub with long straight branches. Golden-yellow flowers in summer are followed by handsome black seed pods.

Buckthorn *Rhamnus catharticus* (P)
Height: 18ft/6m.
Season: Summer, autumn.
Environment: Hedgerow; sunny border.
A dediduous shrub: the tiny greenish-yellow flowers are followed by red and then black berries. Traditionally, the berries yield yellow dye when unripe and green dye when ripe.

Bulbous Buttercup *Ranunculus bulbosus* (P)
Height: 6–18in/15–45cm.
Season: Summer.
Environment: Meadow.
A hairy plant with marked, swollen base to stem. The familiar bright yellow flowers have shiny undersides. This is a species that prefers dry, calcareous soils.

Burnet Rose *Rosa pimpinellifolia* (P)
Height: 6in–2ft/15–60cm.
Season: Summer, autumn.
Environment: Sunny border.
Low-growing thicket-forming shrub. Sweet-scented creamy white flowers are followed by purplish-black hips in autumn.

Burnet-saxifrage *Pimpinella saxifrage* (P)
Height: 1–3ft/30–90cm.
Season: Summer.
Environment: Sunny border; meadow.
Tall slender plant with umbrella-shaped flower heads covered in white flowers. Distinct sweetish smell is very attractive.

Bush Vetch *Vicia septium* (P)
Height: 1–3ft/30cm–1m.
Season: Summer.
Environment: Sunny border; meadow; hedge row.
Pretty sprawling plant with rounded flower heads which hold up to six bluish-purple blooms.

Carline Thistle *Carlina vulgaris* (B)
Height: 4in–2ft/10–60cm.
Season: Summer, autumn.
Environment: Meadow; hedgerow; wall.
Makes a prickly rosette of leaves for the first year, then straw-coloured flower heads and prickly stemmed leaves in the second. Flowers expand to look like sun-rays in dry weather and close up when the day is damp.

Cat's-ear *Hypochoeris radicata* (P)
Height: 8in–2ft/20–60cm.
Season: Summer.
Environment: Meadow; hedgerow; wall.
A plant similar to dandelions and which spreads equally quickly. It has glowing yellow flowers, wiry stems and rough hairy leaves that are edible.

Chalk Milkwort *Polygala calcarea* (P)
Height: 2–8in/5–20cm.
Season: Summer.
Environment: Meadow; sunny border; wall.
This is an unusual plant with distinctive grey-green leaves, above which grow short stiff spikes of ice-blue flowers.

Chamomile *Chamaemelum nobile* (P)
Height: 4–12in/10–30cm.
Season: Summer.
Environment: Sunny border; wall.

Vigorously spreading, chamomile makes a mass of daisy-like white flower heads with yellow centres among pretty feathery foliage. Leaves have a pleasant scent of apples and the flower heads can be used for a relaxing and refreshing herbal tea.

Chives *Allium schoenoprasum* (P)
Height: 6–16in/15–40cm.
Season: Summer.
Environment: Sunny border; wall.
This onion flavoured herb produces purple pompon-like flower heads on narrow stems and narrow cylindrical leaves that grow from the base of the plant.

Common Bird's-foot-trefoil *Lotus corniculatus* (P)
Height: 4in–2½ft/10–70cm.
Season: Summer, early autumn.
Environment: Sunny border; meadow.
Trifoliate leaves are very attractive. Yellow flowers may be streaked with red. This low-lying/creeping plant dislikes very acidic soils.

Common Centaury *Centaurium erythraea* (A)
Height: 1–12in/3–30cm.
Season: Summer, autumn.
Environment: Sunny border; meadow; woodland; hedgerow; wall.
Charming delicate plant varying in size according to where planted. Produces small, soft-pink tubular flowers with yellow centre, and greyish-green foliage.

Common Fumitory *Fumaria officinalis* (A)
Height: 12–20in/30–50cm.
Season: Summer, autumn.
Environment: Sunny border; wall.
Slender feathery leaves which have a bluish-green tinge, and spikes of tubular pink flowers.

Common Knapweed ('Hardheads')
Centaurea nigra (P)
Height: 1–2ft/30–60cm.
Season: Summer, autumn.

Fig 116   The lesser knapweed (Centaurea nigra) has charming spiky pink flowers.

Environment: Sunny border; woodland; meadow; hedgerow.
Colourful thistle-type plant with reddish-purple flowers on globular flower heads. Lance-shaped leaves.

Common Mallow   *Malva sylvestris* (P)
Height: 1–3ft/30–90cm.
Season: Summer, autumn.
Environment: Sunny border; meadow; wall.
Bushy plant with large ivory-shaped leaves and big rose-purple flowers. Can act as a soothing agent for sores and stings.

Common Restharrow   *Ononis repens* (P)
Height: 1–2ft/30–60cm.
Season: Summer, early autumn.
Environment: Sunny border; meadow.
This creeping plant with downy, woody stems and soft spines has pink flowers. Calcareous soils are preferred and it dislikes a damp location.

Common Sea-lavender   *Limonium vulgare* (P)
Height: 4–16in/10–40cm.
Season: Summer, autumn.
Environment: Sunny border; wall.
Tiny bluish-purple flowers are densely packed on branching stems with large greyish leaves. This plant also looks pretty when dried.

Common Sorrel   *Rumex acetosa* (P)
Height: 1–2½ft/30–80cm.
Season: Summer.
Environment: Meadow; woodland; hedgerow.
Glossy, arrow-shaped leaves which turn crimson. Greenish-red papery flowers. The leaves are edible.

Fig 117   Sorrel (Rumex acetosa) is a good-looking, leafy meadow plant that produces russet seed spikes.

Common Vetch *Vicia sativa* (A)
Height: 6in–4ft/15–120cm.
Season: Summer, autumn.
Environment: Hedgerow; meadow.
Short-stalked mauve flowers grow in pairs on stems at the base of each leaf. Later, they produce slightly hairy seed pods. This Vetch can climb other plants up to 4ft(120cm).

Corn Buttercup *Ranunculus arvensis* (A)
Height: 6–20in/15–50cm.
Season: Summer.
Environment: Sunny border; meadow.
The bright yellow flowers are attractive to butterflies. Grow with wild pansies, mayweed, cornflower and corn-cockle for a stunning effect. The ripe seeds are beautiful but poisonous if eaten by humans.

Fig 118 Delightful cowslips for meadow and woodland.

Cowslip *Primula veris*(P)
Height: 4in–1ft/10–30cm.
Season: Spring, summer.
Environment: Sunny border; meadow.
Downy-haired, crinkly, leaves grow at the base of this plant. Flowers are deep yellow or buff with orange spots. It will do well in chalk and will grow in alluvial and clay soils as well as damp to wet calcareous soils.

Creeping Jenny   ('Moneywort')
Lysimachia nummularia (P)
Height: Low and creeping.
Season: Summer, autumn.
Environment: Meadow; wall; sunny border; woodland
A sprawling plant that spreads to produce a dense mat of shining bright-green leaves and vivid yellow cup-shaped flowers.

Fig 119 Creeping Jenny (Lysimachia nummularia) is an excellent ground-cover plant for a wide variety of situations.

Cuckoo Flower *Cardamine pratensis* (P)
Height: 6in–2ft/15–60cm.
Season: Summer.
Environment: Marsh and pond; meadow.
A graceful plant with pinnate leaves and lilac or white flowers. Most soil types are suitable.

Cyclamen (Sow-Bread)
Cyclamen hederifolium (P)
Height: 4–12in/10–30cm.
Season: Autumn.
Environment: Woodland; hedgerow.
Delicate pink or white flowers like tiny butterflies are the distinctive feature of this almost exotic-looking shade-tolerant plant.

Daisy *Bellis perennis* (P)
Height: 3–6in/7–15cm.
Season: Spring, summer, autumn.
Environment: Meadow, sunny border.
Pretty yellow flower heads are surrounded by a ring of white rays, sometimes tinged with pink. Spoon-shaped leaves form a rosette at the base of the plant.

Dame's Violet ('Sweet Rocket')
Hesperis matronalis (P)
Height: 15in–3ft/40–90cm.
Season: Summer.
Environment: Sunny border; meadow.
White or violet flowers become deliciously fragrant towards evening. Sadly a short-lived plant.

Dandelion *Taraxacum officinale* (P)
Height: 2–12in/5–30cm.
Season: Spring, summer, autumn.
Environment: Meadow.
The golden-coloured, sun-like flowers grow on single stalks above a flat rosette of toothed leaves. The flowers are followed in June by 'clocks' – ribbed fruit bearing tiny parachutes of white hairs. Edible leaves. Attractive to bees.

Dog Rose *Rosa canina* (P)
Height: 9ft/3m.

Fig 120 The humble but bright dandelion, Taraxacum officinale.

Season: Summer, autumn.
Environment: Hedgerow.
Large, fragrant pale pink or white flowers are followed in autumn by many flask-shaped, scarlet hips which can be used for medicinal purposes and will attract birds.

Dogwood *Swida sanguinea* syn. (*Cornus sanguinea*) (P)
Height: 12ft/4m.
Season: Summer, autumn.
Environment: Hedgerow.
Hawthorn-scented, white flowers in summer. Clusters of small black berries in September. Leaves and stems turn red in autumn. Inedible berries were once used for lighting lamps.

Dusky Crane's-bill *Geranium phaeum* (P)
Height: 2–3ft/60–90cm.
Season: Summer.
Environment: Sunny border; meadow.
With its unusual deep-purple, almost black flowers, this sunlover provides excellent ground cover.

Dyer's Greenweed *Genista tinctoria* (P)
Height: 1–2½ft/30–70cm.
Season: Summer, autumn.
Environment: Sunny border; wall.
A hardy shrub which thrives in poor soil. It has small glossy leaves and spires of golden-yellow pea flowers which reaveal that it is actually a dwarf form of Broom. A yellow dye can be made from the flowers.

Elder *Sambucus nigra* (P)
Height: 22ft/7m.
Season: Summer, autumn.
Environment: Meadow; woodland.
Small, creamy-white flowers grow in flat-topped masses in early summer and are attractive to insects. Flowers and berries are used for wine-making. Heavy clusters of black elderberries produced in autumn are used for jams and wine-making or eaten by birds.

Elecampane *Inula helenium* (P)
Height: 2–5ft/60–150cm.
Season: Summer.
Environment: Meadow; sunny border; wood land.
Distinguished by its large daisy-shaped flower heads of a rich golden-yellow colour, the plant has branching stems. Lower leaves can grow up to 1ft(30cm) long. Flowers can be used to dye cloth.

Fennel *Foeniculum vulgare* (P)
Height: 4–6ft/1½–2m.
Season: Summer, autumn.
Environment: Meadow; wall.
Tall, green lace-like foliage and masses of tiny yellow flowers make this a handsome herb.

Fig 121   The edible autumn fruits of the elder, Sambucus nigra.

There is also a bronze variety. Leaves, seeds and flowers have a distinctive aniseed aroma and may be used to flavour fish and egg dishes. Attractive to bees and can be used to dye cloth.

Feverfew *Tanacetum parthenium* (P)
Height: 10in–2ft/25–60cm.
Season: Summer.
Environment: Sunny border; hedgerow; meadow.
Daisy-like flower heads grow in clusters above feathery light-green foliage. The plant has a strong pungent smell when crushed and bitter leaves. Attractive to bees.

Field Scabious *Knautia arvensis* (P)
Height: 10in–3ft/25cm–1m.
Season: Summer, early autumn.
Environment: Meadow.
Pin-cushion flower heads, mauve in colour. Can number up to fifty flowers on one flower head. This large attractive plant is a good provider of nectar for bees and butterflies.

Fringed Water-Lily *Nymphoides peltata* (P)
Height: 5ft/1.5m.
Season: Summer, early autumn.
Environment: Marsh and pond.
Likened to a miniature water-lily on account of its round glossy leaves that float on the water surface. The funnel shaped, yellow flowers have distinctive fringed petals that stand just above the water surface.

Frogbit *Hydrocharis morsus-ranae* (P)
Height: 4in/10cm (above water).
Season: Summer.
Environment: Marsh and pond.
Circular leaves form a rosette around small white flowers. Flowers have yellow blotches in the centre. Both leaves and flowers float on the water surface while the stems float horizontally underwater.

Germander Speedwell *Veronica chamaedrys* (P)
Height: 4in–1½ft/10–40cm.
Season: Spring, summer.
Environment: Sunny border; meadow; woodland.
A hairy plant which grows in most soils. Bright blue flower heads with a white eye are especially pretty.

Giant Bellflower *Campanula latifolia* (P)
Height: 2–4ft/60–120cm.
Season: Summer.
Environment: Meadow; woodland; sunny border (shady garden).
Pale blue or white bell-shaped flowers are displayed on tall stems above oval-shaped foliage).

Gipsywort *Lycopus europaeus* (P)
Height: 1–3ft/30cm–1m
Season: Summer, early autumn.
Environment: Sunny border; wall; woodland; marsh and pond.
Deeply toothed leaves on which grow clusters of tiny white or pinkish bell-shaped flowers. Can be used to produce a strong, black dye.

Globeflower *Trollius europaeus* (P)
Height: 4–20in/10–50cm.
Season: Summer.
Environment: Marsh and pond.
This striking damp-soil plant has big, soft, spherical flower heads similar to a buttercup, only much larger and glossier.

Goat's Beard ('Jack-Go-To-Bed-At-Noon' or 'Field Salsify') *Tragopogon pratensis* (B)
Height: 1–2ft/30–70cm.
Season: Summer.
Environment: Sunny border; meadow.
The yellow, dandelion-like flowers, open early in the day and close at noon. Long grass-like leaves. Round balls of fruits develop after flowering, covered in tufts of long, silky hairs similar to dandelion 'clocks', only longer lasting. The root (similar to parsnip) and leaves are edible.

Goldenrod *Solidago virgaurea* (P)
Height: 1–2ft/30–60cm.
Season: Summer, early autumn.
Environment: Sunny border; meadow; woodland.
Rapidly spreading, this clump-forming plant produces bright yellow flowers which appear in summer in sprays. Sharply-pointed hoary leaves on branched stems. Once used as herbal remedy to treat internal and external wounds.

Greater Bird's-foot-trefoil *Lotus uliginosus* (P)
Height: 1–2ft/30–60cm.
Season: Summer, early autumn.
Environment: Marsh and pond.
The deep yellow flowers are larger than those of common bird's-foot-trefoil and appear without the touch of red of other bird's-foot-trefoils. Broad, dark-green leaves.

Greater Knapweed *Centauria scabiosa* (P)
Height: 1–3ft/30–90cm.
Season: Summer, early autumn.
Environment: Meadow.
Stiff, grooved stems support pinnately lobed, bristly leaves. Reddish-purple flowers. The plant

prefers calcareous soils but will grow on basic clays. It is particularly suited to chalk or limestone soils.

Great Mullein   *Verbascum thapsus* (B)
Height: 1–6ft/30cm–2m.
Season: Summer.
Environment: Sunny border.
Tall spikes of densely packed yellow flowers appear above large downy leaves and are attractive to bees. Leaves attract caterpillars of the mullein moth. Once used as herbal remedy for bronchial disorders, and yellow hair dye can be made from the flowers. During first year of growth, a large rosette of woolly leaves develops and the familiar long flower stem is produced the following season.

Ground Ivy   *Glechoma hederacea* (P)
Height: 4–12in/10–30cm.
Season: Spring, summer.
Environment: Sunny border; meadow; wood land.
Leaves are dainty and kidney shaped on this useful ground-cover plant. It has small, mauve, lavender-like flowers and the leaves have a pungent, minty scent. Once used for making ales and also for medicinal purposes.

Hare's-foot Clover   *Trifolium arvense* (A)
Height: 4–8in/10–20cm.
Season: Summer, autumn.
Environment: Sunny border; wall.
Soft, downy flower heads are creamy coloured with a pinkish tinge. Trefoil leaves are mat-forming. Attractive to bees and butterflies.

Hawthorn   *Crataegus monogyna* (P)
Height: 15ft/5m.
Season: Summer, autumn, winter.
Environment: Meadow; hedgerow.
Has white blossom in early summer and red berries in autumn. The flowers are strongly sweet-smelling. The shrub itself is very tough and thorny and grows quickly, making it an excellent hedgerow plant.

Heather   *Calluna vulgaris* (P)
Height: 2ft/60cm.
Season: Summer, autumn.
Environment: Sunny border; woodland.
Attractive evergreen plant with small, pinky-purple flowers that form loose spikes at the tops of the stems. Leaves are small and cover the many stems all year. Provides food for bees, butterflies and caterpillars.

Hedge Bedstraw   *Galium mollugo* (P)
Height: 1½–3ft/45cm–1m.
Season: Summer, autumn.
Environment: Sunny border; hedgerow; woodland.
With its fine, pointed leaves and small white flowers, this common plant was once used in cheese-making, and the roots can produce a red dye.

Hedge Woundwort   *Stachys sylvatica* (P)
Height: 1–3ft/30cm–1m.
Season: Summer.
Environment: Meadow; woodland; hedgerow.
Tall, hairy plant with loose spikes of purple-brown flowers above heart-shaped leaves. A good bee plant. Originally used as a herbal remedy for wounds and to stem bleeding. Leaves contain volatile oil with antiseptic properties.

Hoary Plantain   *Plantago media* (P)
Height: 6–12in/15–30cm.
Season: Summer.
Environment: Sunny border; meadow.
Pale pink or white fluffy flowers from oval flower heads on long stalks. A flat rosette of leaves, covered in white hairs grows at the base. Delicately scented and very attractive to bees and caterpillars.

Holly   *Ilex aquifolium* (P)
Height: 10–36ft/3–12m.
Season: Spring, summer, autumn, winter.
Environment: Hedgerow.
Spiny, evergreen leaves are slow growing but may in time produce clusters of small white flowers in summer and scarlet berries in winter. Birds love

the berries and the holly blue butterfly also feeds from it.

Honesty *Lunaria annua* (B)
Height: 3ft/1m.
Season: Summer.
Environment: Sunny border; meadow; wood land.
The loose, fragrant clusters of flowers are either brilliant purple or white in colour. They are followed by fruits that split to reveal almost transparent membranes. These are popular with flower arrangers when dried. Very attractive to butterflies and caterpillars of the orange-tip butterfly.

Hop *Humulus lupulus* (P)
Height: 18ft/6m.
Season: Summer, autumn.
Environment: Meadow, woodland, hedgerow.
Male and female plants look quite different. The male has yellowish flowers that grow in branched clusters. The female produces tiny, green, scented flowers and yields globular, greenish fruits in autumn.

Horseshoe Vetch *Hippocrepis comosa* (P)
Height: 4–16in/10–40cm.
Season: Summer.
Environment: Meadow.
A trailing, low-growing plant with pretty, golden-yellow pea flowers occasionally striped with red. Similar to bird's-foot-trefoil except that the leaves are arranged in rows of leaflets and the seed pods are horseshoe shaped. A colourful plant, attractive to bees and a food provider for caterpillars of the adonis blue butterfly.

Hound's Tongue *Cynoglossum officinale* (B)
Height: 1–3ft/30–90cm.
Season: Summer.
Environment: Meadow.
A tall, plant with small funnel-shaped, crimson flowers and soft, downy, grey leaves. It has a distinctive odour and is an important nectar plant for bees and butterflies. Once used as a poultice

Fig 122 There is a white form of honesty (Lunaria annua) *which is very pretty amongst the natural greens of a wild garden.*

herb, the hard seed cases look like miniature hedgehogs.

Ivy *Hedera helix* (P)
Height: 100ft/30m.
Season: Winter.
Environment: Woodland; wall; hedgerow.
Evergreen climbing plant that grows up walls, trees and hedges. Leaves are dark green and glossy. Yellowish-green flowers produce globular flower heads. Black berries in winter.

Ivy-leaved Toadflax *Cymbalaria muralis* (P)
Height: 4in–3½ft/10–75cm.
Season: Summer.
Environment: Hedgerow, wall.
A creeper with glossy ivy-shaped leaves and lilac, snapdragon-like flowers with a yellow centre. There is also a white variety. A good nectar plant for bees.

Jacob's Ladder *Polemonium caeruleum* (P)
Height: 1–3ft/30–90cm.
Season: Summer.
Environment: Sunny border; woodland; hedgerow; wall.
Cobalt blue or white flowers and bright green foliage. Very rare – only found in the north of England.

Fig 123 Jacob's ladder (Polemonium caeruleum) makes tall spikes of mauve blooms above a dense bush of feathery foliage.

Kidney Vetch *Anthyllis vulneraria* (P)
Height: 9–12in/25–30cm.
Season: Summer.
Environment: Sunny border; wall.
Large, rounded flower heads with downy yellow flowers and pale green, silky leaves make this a very pretty plant. Flowers can vary from cream to crimson. It is a rich source of nectar for bees, and butterflies lay their eggs on the plant. Main source of food for the small blue butterfly.

Lady-Fern *Athyrium filix-femina* (P)
Height: 8in–3ft/20cm–1m (fronds).
Season: Spring, summer, autumn.
Environment: Woodland; meadow.
This has a delicate texture with a graceful feathery appearance and forms distinctive clumps.

Lady's Bedstraw *Galium verum* (P)
Height: 6in–3ft/15cm–1m.
Season: Summer.
Environment: Meadow.
With golden-yellow flowers, and thread-like leaves, the plant spreads by means of underground runners. Produces a yellow or red dye used to curdle or colour milk for cheese-making.

Lady's Mantle ('Lion's Foot')
Alchemilla vulgaris (P)
Height: 6–8in/15–45cm.
Season: Summer, autumn.
Environment: Meadow.
A low-growing herb which makes attractive ground cover. Distinctive pale green leaves and loose clusters of tiny yellowish-green flowers.

Larkspur *Delphinium ambiguum*
(syn *Consolida ambigua*) (A)
Height: 1–2ft/30–60cm.
Season: Summer.
Environment: Sunny border, meadow.
The naturalised variety is smaller than the cultivated version. Elegant, with loose spikes of intense purplish-blue flowers above feathery, fern-like leaves, the plant is very attractive to butterflies and other insects.

Lesser Calamint *Calamintha nepeta* (P)
Height: 1–2ft/30–60cm.
Season: Summer, autumn.
Environment: Sunny border; meadow.
Tiny, delicate, pale mauve flowers on pale grey stems and leaves that are covered in fine, downy hair make this a pretty plant. It has an aromatic scent which attracts butterflies. Nectar from the flowers also attracts bees.

Lesser Stitchwort *Stellaria graminea* (P)
Height: 6in–2ft/15–60cm.
Season: Summer.
Environment: Meadow; hedgerow.
Tiny white flowers with yellow centres are scattered among the foliage. It tends to be straggly, often using other plants for support.

Lesser Trefoil *Trifolium dubium* (A)
Height: 2–10in/5–25cm.
Season: Summer, autumn.
Environment: Sunny border; meadow.
Low and creeping this short-lived plant survives by seeding. It often turns purplish in colour and the flowers are yellow, turning brown. Grows best in open vegetation on all soil types.

Maidenhair Spleenwort
Asplenium trichomanes (P)
Height: 2–14in/5–35cm.
Season: Spring, summer, autumn, winter.
Environment: Wall.
A decorative fern with a fine feathery appearance. Neat pairs of leaves grow along the length of black hair-like stems.

Maiden Pink *Dianthus deltoides* (P)
Height: 6in–1½ft/15–45cm.
Season: Summer, autumn.
Environment: Sunny border; wall.
Low-spreading plant forming a mat of grey-green foliage. In summer, a mass of rose-red flowers, delicately freckled with pale spots, appear. They have no scent but their bright colouring attracts insects. Dull weather causes flowers to close.

Marsh Mallow *Althaea officinalis* (P)
Height: 2–4ft/60–120cm.
Season: Summer, autumn.
Environment: Sunny border; marsh and pond.
Tall and stately in appearance, the plant produces large, pale pink flowers which grow in clusters from the upper part of the stem. Velvety leaves appear slightly folded, almost like a fan. Roots have been used for various pains and swellings. It was also used traditionally to make marshmallow sweets. Flowers attract butterflies.

Meadow Buttercup *Ranunculus acris* (P)
Height: 6in–3½ft/15cm–1m.
Season: Summer.
Environment: Meadow.
Deeply cut, palmate leaves, hairy stems and bright yellow, glossy flowers are one of the most familiar meadow sights. It likes neutral or calcareous soils.

Meadow Crane's-bill *Geranium pratense* (P)
Height: 1–1½ft/30–80cm.
Season: Summer, early autumn.
Environment: Meadow; sunny border.
Stout and handsome, the stems are often reddish, with violet-blue flowers. Dislikes very acidic soils but likes damp soil. Often takes at least four years from seed to flower, so needs patience.

Meadow Vetchling *Lathyrus pratensis* (P)
Height: 1–4ft/30–120cm.
Season: Summer.
Environment: Meadow.
Slender, leafy plant with small, yellow pea flowers. Attractive to bees and butterflies, this is a scrambling plant that forms clumps.

Mezereon *Daphne mezereum* (P)
Height: 1½–3ft/50cm–1m.
Season: Spring, summer.
Environment: Woodland, meadow.
Slow-growing upright bush with flowers early in the season. Very rare and especially protected in the wild. Tiny, rosy-pink, tubular-shaped flowers grow in clusters up the stems before the leaves appear. Bright scarlet, poisonous berries.

Milk Thistle *Silybum marianum* (B)
Height: 3–5ft/1–1½m.
Season: Summer.
Environment: Sunny border.
With handsome, large, purple flower heads and white-veined, spiky leaves, this plant can be naturalized. The first season of its two-year cycle produces a low rosette of white-veined leaves, and bees and butterflies are attracted to the colourful flower heads in the second year.

Monk's Hood (Aconite) *Aconitum napellus* (P)
Height: 3–5ft/1–1½m.
Season: Summer, autumn.
Environment: Summer border; meadow; woodland.
Striking plant with tall purple-blue spires of hood-shaped flowers and attractive, finger-shaped foliage. Very attractive to bumble-bees. It is still important in homeopathic medicine but extremely poisonous.

Moschatel ('Townhall clock')
Adoxa moschatellina (P)
Height: 2–6in/5–15cm.
Season: Summer.
Environment: Sunny border; meadow; woodland.
This small, spreading plant has delicate, yellowish-green flowers and pale green leaves. The musk-like scent becomes stronger at dusk and in damp weather and attracts insects. The flowers are arranged on the stem in an unusual cube-like shape.

Mountain Pansy *Viola lutea* (P)
Height: Low.
Season: Summer.
Environment: Wall.
With large, bright yellow flowers, sometimes purple-violet, this pretty alpine forms mats of foliage.

Mouse-Ear Hawkweed
Hieracium pilosella (P)
Height: 2in–1ft/5–30cm.

Season: Summer, autumn.
Environment: Sunny border; meadow.
A small, spreading plant which spreads rapidly by means of runners. Bright lemon-yellow flower heads, similar to those of the dandelion, are streaked with red underneath. The single flowering stems rise above a rosette of lobe-shaped leaves. The plant is covered with white hairs and was once used to treat jaundice.

Musk Mellow *Malva moschata* (P)
Height: 1–3ft/30–85cm.
Season: Summer.
Environment: Meadow; woodland.
This graceful plant has rose-pink or white flowers. It likes a moderately fertile soil.

Musk Thistle (Nodding Thistle) *Carduus nutans* (B)
Height: 9in–3ft/20cm–1m.
Season: Summer.
Environment: Sunny border; meadow.
Distinguished by the big, drooping, reddish-purple flowers, this thistle has long spiky stems and leaves. The cup-shaped flower heads are backed by small spines. Its strong musky odour attracts butterflies as well as some seed-eating birds.

Narrow-leaved Everlasting Pea
Lathyrus sylvestris (P)
Height: 3–9ft/1–3m.
Season: Summer.
Environment: Sunny border; meadow; hedge row.
Closely related to the sweet pea, the small, buff-yellow flowers are flushed pink. As its name suggests, the leaves are long and narrow.

Ox-eye Daisy *Chrysanthemum leucanthemum* (P)
Height: 8in–2½ft/20–70cm.
Season: Summer.
Environment: Sunny border; meadow; marsh and pond.
Large plant with small, glossy leaves and cheery

white flowers with yellow centres. Dislikes very acid clays or sands.

Parsley Fern *Cryptogramma crispa* (P)
Height: 6–8in/15–20cm.
Season: Spring, autumn.
Environment: Sunny border, meadow, wood land.
A fern with decorative feathery fronds resembling the herb parsley. Will not grow in alkaline soils.

Perennial Flax *Linum anglicum* (syn. *L. perenne*) (P)
Height: 1–2ft/30–60cm.
Season: Summer.
Environment: Sunny border; meadow.
A tufted plant with numerous small leaves and sky-blue flowers on thin, waving stems.

Pheasant's Eye *Adonis annua* (A)
Height: 4in–1½ft/10–40cm.
Season: Summer.
Environment: Sunny border.
Known for its scarlet flowers with dark centres like red buttercups and feathery leaves, their brilliant colour attracts butterflies. Regarded as a weed in southern Europe this is, in fact, a rare and declining species that only grows in alkaline soil.

Fig 124 Pheasant's eye (Adonis annua) *is one of the loveliest wild flowers and a traditional cornfield plant.*

Pignut *Conopodium majus* (P)
Height: 10–12in/25–50cm.
Season: Summer.
Environment: Woodland; hedgerow.
Delicate umbrellas of pretty, white flowers grow in clusters on branched flower heads. Finely divided leaves are similar to, but darker than those of the wild carrot. It is related to the carrot family and its grown tuberous roots are edible.

Purple Saxifrage *Saxifraga oppositifolia* (P)
Height: Creeping and mat-forming
Season: Spring, summer.
Environment: Sunny border; meadow.
This sprawling plant flowers in brilliant profusion in early spring. The small, starry flowers range from pink to deep purple on trailing wiry stems with tiny leaves.

Purple Toadflax *Linaria purpurea* (P)
Height: 2–3ft/60cm–1m.
Season: Summer.
Environment: Sunny border; meadow.
Slender spikes of bright violet, snapdragon-like flowers and short, narrow leaves which are delicate but attractive.

Fig 125 The long purple flower-spikes of Linaria purpurea.

Fig 126 Ramsons (Allium ursinum) *produce a strong onion scent.*

Ragged-robin *Lychnis flos-cuculi* (P)
Height: 1–2½ft/30–75cm.
Season: Summer.
Environment: Sunny border; meadow; marsh and pond.
A delicate looking plant with pointed leaves and rose-red, rarely white spiky flowers. Prefers damp or wet soils.

Ramsons ('Wild garlic') *Allium ursinum* (P)
Height: 1–1½ft/30–45cm.
Season: Summer.
Environment: Meadow; woodland.
Clusters of snow-white flowers appear on long stalks above broad, bright green leaves in shady areas. Easy to notice by its distinctive onion-like smell.

112

Red Clover *Trifolium pratense*
Height: 4in–2ft/10–60cm.
Season: Summer, early autumn.
Environment: Sunny border; meadow.
This slightly downy plant produces pinkish-purple flowers. It will tolerate all but the most acid soils.

Red Dead-nettle *Lamium purpureum* (A)
Height: 4–18in/10–45cm.
Season: Spring, summer, autumn.
Environment: Sunny border; meadow; wall.
Pinkish-purple flowers are slightly hooded and grown in small clusters. The heart-shaped purplish leaves emit a pungent smell when crushed. This is an important, early season bee and butterfly nectar plant.

Red Valerian *Centranthus ruber* (P)
Height: 1–3ft/30–90cm.
Season: Summer.
Environment: Sunny border; wall.
These bushy, greyish-green plants have large, branched flower heads of deep red. The elegant, fragrant flowers are very attractive to butterflies. Flowers can also be all shades of pink and white.

Ribbed Melilot *Melilotus officinalis* (B)
Height: 1–4ft/30–120cm.
Season: Summer, autumn.
Environment: Sunny border; meadow.
Long spikes of small yellow flowers which attract bees and caterpillars. Once used for making poultices, the plant gives off the smell of new-mown hay when it dries.

Rock Cinquefoil *Potentilla rupestris* (P)
Height: 8–20in/20–50cm.
Season: Summer.
Environment: Wall.
A rare, native plant with large, white, strawberry-like flowers which grow in loose clusters on branching stems.

Rough Chervil *Chaerophyllum temulentum* (B)
Height: 1–3ft/30–90cm.
Season: Summer.

Fig 127 *A traditional meadow flower: Red clover,* Trifolium pratense.

Environment: Sunny border; meadow; hedge-row.
This delicate version of cow parsley has big, umbrella-shaped flower heads of tiny white flowers. Attractive foliage features purple-spotted stems. It is a late flowerer and poisonous.

Rough Hawkbit *Leontodon hispidus* (P)
Height: 4in–2ft/10–60cm.
Season: Summer, early autumn.
Environment: Sunny border; meadow.
A rough, hairy plant, its dandelion-like, yellow flower heads, are orange or reddish beneath. Calcareous or neutral soils are preferred.

Royal Fern *Osmunda regalis* (P)
Height: 3–6ft/1–2m.
Season: Spring, summer, autumn.
Environment: Marsh and pond, woodland.
One of the most magnificent ferns, the buff-pink elegant fronds have cream streaks. Fronds are a perfect clear green colour when mature, and in autumn, turn to gold and red-brown. It will grow into dense bushy clumps.

Sainfoin *Onobrychis viciifolia* (P)
Height: 4in–2½ft/l0–80cm.
Season: Summer.
Environment: Sunny border; meadow.
A bushy plant with cone-shaped spikes, the flowers are bright pink and streaked with red. It has vetch-like leaves which are attractive to bees. The beautiful seeds are worth examining under a magnifying glass.

Salad Burnet *Poterium sanguisorba* (syn. *Sanguisorba minor*) (P)
Height: 9in–1½ft/20–45cm.
Season: Summer.
Environment: Sunny border; meadow.
An attractive plant with greenish-red pompon-like flower heads and tiny, intricate, evergreen foliage. Bruised leaves emit a pleasant perfume and taste of cucumber. Can be used in salads and sauces. Deep-rooting herb which is very drought-resistant.

Saw-wort *Serratula tinctoria* (P)
Height: 8in–2½ft/20–80cm.
Season: Summer, autumn.
Environment: Sunny border; meadow; hedge-row.
Similar to a small knapweed, the purplish-pink, fluffy flower heads are arranged on branching stems. The plant is now becoming scarce in the wild. It was once used as a herbal remedy for wounds and a yellow-green dye is produced when leaves are mixed with Alum.

Scarlet Pimpernel *Anagallis arvensis* (A)
Height: Low and spreading.
Season: Summer.
Environment: Sunny border; wall.
Small and delicate with bright, starry flowers, these are usually red although rare blue and pink forms exist. Shiny, oval-shaped leaves with a pointed tip grow in pairs. Neither nectar-producing nor scented so visited by few insects.

Fig 128 The scarlet pimpernel (Anagallis arvensis) *is a pretty ground-cover plant with tiny red flowers.*

Fig 129 The bright flowers of scarlet pimpernel, Anagallis arvensis.

Scented Mayweed ('German Chamomile') *Matricaria recutita* (syn. *Chamomilla recutita*) (A)
Height: 4–20in/10–50cm.
Season: Summer.
Environment: Sunny border; meadow.
Finer than other mayweeds and the first to flower, the scented mayweed produces smaller, daisy-like flowers which have a very strong, sweet scent. Traditionally used for soothing children's teething pains.

Scentless Mayweed *Tripleurospermum inodorum* (syn. *Matricaria perforata*) (A)
Height: 6in–2ft/15–60cm.
Season: Summer, autumn.
Environment: Sunny border; meadow.
With large, daisy-like flower heads and delicate thread-like leaves, this adaptable plant grows in most soils. It is regarded as a common weed and finishes flowering around the end of July.

Sea Campion *Silene maritima* (P)
Height: 6–8in/15–20cm.
Season: Summer.
Environment: Wall.
Small, glaucous, waxy leaves form neat, spreading cushions. The short stalks bear large, white flowers, which have cylindrical inflated calyces (smaller than those of the bladder campion to which it is related).

Sea Holly *Eryngium maritimum* (P)
Height: 1–3ft/30–90cm.
Season: Summer.
Environment: Sunny border; wall.
Tiny, metallic-blue flowers crowd a thistle-like flower head. Spiny, bluish-green leaves are edged with white. Roots used to be candied and sold as an aphrodisiac.

Sea Wormwood *Artemisia maritima* (P)
Height: 8–20in/20–50cm.
Season: Summer, autumn.
Environment: Sunny border; wall.
This finely textured, spreading plant makes an attractive silver bush. Small, dark-gold flowers appear in sprays above intricate foliage. Very aromatic. Dust-like seeds.

Fig 130 The sea wormwood (Artemesia maritima) has silver foliage and requires a well-drained soil.

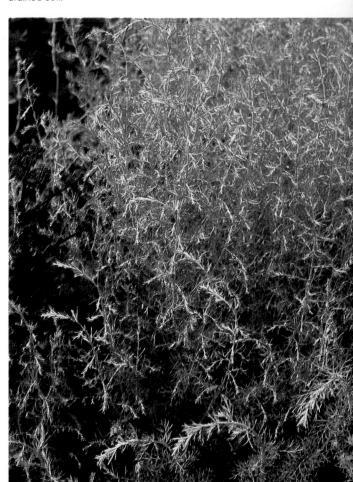

Fig 131 Self-heal (Prunella vulgaris) is an excellent butterfly plant for meadows and borders.

Selfheal *Prunella vulgaris* (P)
Height: 2in–1ft/5–30cm.
Season: Summer, early autumn.
Environment: Sunny border, meadow.
Short, creeping and downy, the flowers are violet to pink. Basic or neutral soils are preferred.

Sheep's Bit *Jasione montana* (B)
Height: 2–20in/5–50cm.
Season: Summer.
Environment: Sunny border; wall.
This sometimes sprawling plant has dense, powder-blue flower heads that resemble pincushions and small leaves that emit a strong smell when bruised. Likes an acid soil.

Silver Hair-grass *Aira caryophyllea* (A)
Height: 2–12in/5–30cm.
Season: Summer.
Environment: Sunny border; wall.
Light and delicate in appearance, the tiny flower heads give a misty impression. An attractive native grass.

Silver Weed *Potentilla anserina* (P)
Height: Low and creeping.
Season: Summer.
Environment: Meadow; sunny border; wall.
Glossy, silvery leaves with hairy undersides are as pretty as the rose-like yellow flowers. Leaves and roots are edible (enjoyed especially by geese). Herbalists use the root for sore throats and mouth ulcers.

Slender Speedwell *Veronica filiformis* (P)
Height: Creeping and mat-forming.
Season: Spring, summer.
Environment: Meadow.
The plant spreads rapidly and produces attractive blue flowers with a white lower lip. Similar to but smaller than germander speedwell with small kidney-shaped leaves.

Smooth Tare *Vicia tetrasperma* (A)
Height: 8–12in/20–30cm.
Season: Summer, autumn.
Environment: Sunny border; meadow.
An attractive foliage plant with 3–6 pairs of bright green, slender leaves. Flowers are very small and rich lilac in colour. Seed pods always contain four seeds, unlike hairy tare, which is two seeded.

Soapwort *Saponaria officinalis* (P)
Height: 1–2ft/30–60cm.
Season: Summer, autumn.
Environment: Meadow, sunny border; wall.
A tall plant which has a tendency to sprawl without support, produces showy, flesh-pink flowers in compact clusters and pale green leaves. Boiled roots and leaves were once used to wash wool as they produce a gentle soapy lather.

Spindle *Euonymus europaeus* (P)
Height: 18ft/6m.
Season: Summer, autumn, winter.
Environment: Hedgerow, woodland.
A deciduous bush with small green flowers in loose clusters. The simple pointed leaves turn bronze in autumn. The deep pink fruits split to reveal bright orange berries, which are poisonous to humans.

Spiny Restharrow *Ononis spinosa* (P)
Height: 12–16in/30–40cm.
Season: Summer, autumn.
Environment: Hedgerow, meadow.
A shrubby plant with purple-pink flowers in summer, spiny stems and small green leaves. It looks similar to common restharrow. A good food plant for caterpillars.

Fig 132 Soapwort (Saponaria) *is a pretty plant for bank or border.*

Spring Squill *Scilla verna* (P)
Height: 2–6in/5–15cm.
Season: Spring, summer.
Environment: Meadow; sunny border.
Making clusters of star-shaped bluish-violet flowers with green grass-like leaves, the flowers are followed by distinctive black globular seed pods. It takes several years to flower from seed.

Square-stalked St John's-wort *Hypericum tetrapterum* (P)
Height: 1–2½ft/30–70cm.
Season: Summer, autumn.
Environment: Marsh and pond; meadow.
The plant is very similar to Perforate St John's-wort except that the flowers have an orange centre and the stem is square, not rounded.

Star of Bethlehem *Ornithogalum umbellatum* (P)
Height: 4–12in/10–30cm.
Season: Summer.
Environment: Sunny border; meadow.
Star-shaped, white flowers with a green stripe down the back of each petal are particularly beautiful. Sadly they are light-sensitive and only open in sunny weather.

Stinking Iris ('Gladdon') *Iris foetidissima* (P)
Height: 1–2½ft/30–80cm.
Season: Summer, autumn.
Environment: Sunny border; meadow; woodland.
The small, purple flowers are tinged with yellow, the evergreen leaves sword-like. Glowing, reddish-orange seeds are displayed throughout the winter. Leaves apparently smell of raw beef when crushed giving rise to its common name.

Summer Snowflake *Leucojum aestivum* (P)
Height: 1–2ft/30–60cm.
Season: Summer.
Environment: Marsh and pond.
Gracefully bell-shaped, the white flowers are tinged with green. Leaves are spiky and narrow.

Tansy   *Tanacetum vulgare* (P)
Height: 1–4ft/30–120cm.
Season: Summer, autumn.
Environment: Sunny border; woodland.
Disc-shaped flower heads with golden-yellow flowers and dark green, lacy, very aromatic foliage are attractive to bees. Yellow dye is made from the flowers. There is a garden variety with shorter, crisper leaves. Once a popular herb, the leaves were used to flavour egg dishes and buns.

Thrift   *Armeria maritima* (P)
Height: 4–8in/10–20cm.
Season: Summer.
Environment: Sunny border; meadow; woodland.
Forming a carpet of rose-pink or white, starry flowers, the dense, rounded flower heads rise on long stalks above rosettes of narrow, fleshy leaves. Honey scented and a good nectar plant for butterflies.

Tormentil   *Potentilla erecta* (P)
Height: 2–20in/5–50cm.
Season: Summer, autumn.
Environment: Meadow; marsh and pond (peat).
Buttercup-like flowers grow on branching stems and are golden-yellow in colour. Pollinated by insects in warm weather although self-pollinating at night or when the weather is wet. Red dye can be obtained from its roots. Has astringent properties and can be used for tanning leather.

Tree Mallow   *Lavatera arborea* (P)
Height: 2–9ft/60cm–3m.
Season: Summer, autumn.
Environment: Wall.
Bushy and closely covered with crinkled, downy leaves, the large, pinkish-purple mallow flowers appear in summer. Stems become woody like a small tree. This is a plant that requires shelter.

Tutsan   *Hypericum androsaemum* (P)
Height: 16in–3ft/40cm–1m.
Season: Summer, autumn.
Environment: Woodland.

A shrubby, semi-evergreen with yellow flowers in summer followed in autumn by fleshy, red fruits that turn black as they ripen. Handsome autumn foliage.

Vervain   *Verbena officinallis* (P)
Height: 1–3ft/30–90cm.
Season: Summer, autumn.
Environment: Sunny, border.
A bushy plant with rough stalks, the tiny, lilac-coloured flowers are carried on long, slender spikes above grey-green leaves. This plant will grow well in pots and is said to possess both medicinal and magical powers. Indeed it is a staple herb of the medical herbalist, curing a number of ills.

Wallflower   *Cheiranthus cheiri* (P)
Height: 8in–2ft/20–60cm.
Season: Spring–autumn intermittently.
Environment: Sunny border; wall.
Dense spikes of rich yellow flowers have a heady aroma. The leaves are star-shaped. A short-lived plant although it self-seeds readily throughout summer.

Wall Germander   *Teucrium chamaedrys* (P)
Height: 4–8in/10–20cm.
Season: Summer, autumn.
Environment: Sunny border; wall; woodland.
Small and bushy, the evergreen leaves are a shiny, dark-green. Rosy-pink flowers are carried on short spikes and appear late. Leaves have a pungent, aromatic scent, especially when crushed.

Water Forget-me-not   *Myosotis scorpioides* (P)
Height: 6–12in/15–30cm.
Season: Summer, autumn.
Environment: Marsh and pond.
Producing a mass of clear blue flowers with yellow centres and long pointed leaves, the plant spreads rapidly. As the name suggests, the roots of this pretty plant should always be kept moist.

*Fig 133 A brilliant and early display from a clump of wallflowers
(Cheiranthus cheiri).*

Fig 134 *The stunning yellow flowers of the prolific and self-seeding Welsh poppy,* Meconopsis cambrica.

Water-plantain *Alisma plantago-aquatica* (P)
Height: 1–3ft/30cm–1m.
Season: Summer.
Environment: Marsh and pond.
Broad, green leaves provide lush foliage all year round. The tall flower-spikes are covered by tiny white flowers, but are light-sensitive and only open for a few hours each afternoon.

Wavy Hair-grass *Deschampsia flexuosa* (P)
Height: 2–6ft/50cm–2m.
Season: Summer.
Environment: Sunny border; meadow.
This tuft-forming grass spreads by means of rhizomes. Delicate rose-pink flower heads appear on wavy branches and look like pink mist from a distance.

Wayfaring-tree *Viburnum lantana* (P)
Height: 6–18ft/2–6m.
Season: Summer, autumn.
Environment: Woodland; hedgerow.
Creamy flowers form in rounded clusters; the foliage is felted and grey-green. Flowers are followed by bunches of green berries which turn red and finally glossy black when ripe. A good value small tree or hedgerow plant.

Weld *Reseda luteola* (B)
Height: 2–5ft/50cm–1½m.
Season: Summer.
Environment: Woodland; hedgerow; wall.
A rosette of leaves is produced in the first year, from which grows a flower spike of small yellow flowers by the second year. Flowers produce bright yellow dye. The leaves are long and narrow.

Welsh Poppy *Meconopsis cambrica* (P)
Height: 1–2ft/30–60cm.
Season: Summer.
Environment: Meadow; wall.
Delicate and bushy, the papery, bright yellow flowers and light green foliage grow profusely to great effect.

White Bryony *Bryonia dioica* (P)
Height: 10ft/3m.
Season: Summer, autumn.
Environment: Woodland; hedgerow; wall.
This is a useful climber that will grow rapidly through shrubs and trees or over fence and trellis by means of spiral tendrils. Small clusters of flowers, white with a hint of green, are produced in summer, which bees visit frequently. Flowers are followed by strings of orange, yellow and red berries in the autumn, poisonous to both humans and animals.

White Campion *Silene alba* (P)
Height: 1–3ft/30cm–1m.
Season: Summer.
Environment: Sunny border; meadow.
Flowers are delicate and white and give off a faint

scent after dusk. Related to red campion, they will often interbreed if grown together to produce flowers in varying shades of pink. Grow in a large clump for best effect.

White Clover *Trifolium repens* (P)
Height: 2–8in/5–20cm.
Season: Summer, autumn.
Environment: Meadow.
White or rosy flowers grow in loose clusters among trefoil leaves. Often regarded as a garden weed it spreads quickly via creeping stems. Supplies bees with nectar.

White Horehound *Marrubium vulgare* (P)
Height: 1–2ft/30–60cm.
Season: Summer, autumn.
Environment: Sunny border; meadow.
Bushy, with clusters of small, white flowers the wrinkled foliage is silver-green and gives the appearance of being frosted. The plant has a musky, spicy odour that attracts bees. It was once used for treating coughs and other chest problems.

Wild Angelica *Angelica sylvestris* (P)
Height: 1–5ft/30cm–½m.
Season: Summer.
Environment: Sunny border, marsh and pond.
Tall flower stalks at the base of which divided leaves grow in clumps. Umbrella-shaped flower heads are made up of tiny white or pale pink flowers and are attractive when dried.

Wild Carrot *Daucous carota* (B)
Height: 1–3½ft/30cm–1m.
Season: Summer.
Environment: Meadow.
Distinguished by its white umbrella-like flower clusters with stalks appearing from the centre and feathery foliage, this is a plant that prefers dry, calcareous soils.

Wild Clary *Salvia horminoides* (P)
Height: 1–3ft/30–90cm.
Season: Summer, autumn.
Environment: Meadow.

The wrinkled, toothed leaves look grey and dusty. Small, blue-violet flowers appear on tall stems and are slightly aromatic. Later large seeds develop.

Wild Mignonette *Reseda lutea* (B/P)
Height: 1–2½ft/30–75cm.
Season: Summer.
Environment: Meadow; hedgerow.
Similar to weld, although shorter, with leaves that are more divided and crinkly; creamy-yellow, fragrant flowers are produced on tall, floppy flower-spikes. Very attractive to bees and butterflies.

Wild Parsnip *Pastinaca sativa* (B)
Height: 1–4ft/30–120cm.
Season: Summer.
Environment: Meadow; hedgerow.
Tall and branching with large umbrella-shaped flower heads, tiny greenish-yellow flowers and felted leaves; this plant has been used as a substitute for the cultivated parsnip in times of shortage.

Wood Avens ('Herb Bennet') *Geum urbanum* (P)
Height: 1–2ft/30–60cm.
Season: Summer.
Environment: Woodland.
Dainty, bright yellow flowers and dark green leaves provide useful ground cover in shady areas. Roots have a delicate aroma similar to cloves and have medicinal properties.

Wood Millet *Milium effusum* (P)
Height: 1½–6ft/45cm–2m.
Season: Summer.
Environment: Meadow; woodland.
Loose tufts support small spikes of green flowers. The plant is used to provide food for game-birds and as an ornamental grass.

Wood Sage ('Garlic Sage')
Teucrium scorodonia (P)
Height: 6in–2ft/15–60cm.

Season: Summer, autumn.
Environment: Sunny border; hedgerow; wood land.
Its decorative foliage and pale greenish-white flowers on one-sided flower-spikes are very attractive. The heart-shaped leaves smell of garlic when crushed and taste of hops (they have been used as a substitute). It was supposed to be good for blood disorders, colds and fever.

Wood Vetch *Vicia sylvatica* (P)
Height: 2–6ft/60cm–2m.
Season: Summer.
Environment: Meadow; woodland; hedgerow.
Producing large, white flowers with marked bluish-purple veins, this is a valuable fodder plant for livestock.

Wormwood *Artemisia absinthium* (P)
Height: 2–4ft/60–120cm.
Season: Summer.
Environment: Sunny border; meadow.
Pretty silvery-grey foliage with a silky texture and the tiny yellow flowers produce a fine display in summer. Very aromatic and repels insects particularly ants. Once used in absinthe for its bitter task – a potent drink banned throughout medieval Europe. Dust-like seed.

Yarrow *Achillea millefolium* (P)
Height: 4in–2½ft/10–70cm.
Season: Summer, early autumn.
Environment: Sunny border; meadow; wood land.
A downy, aromatic plant with white, rose-like flower heads. Will grow on most soils except the most acid.

Yellow Corydalis *Corydalis lutea* (P)
Height: 6–12in/15–30cm.
Season: Summer, autumn.
Environment: Wall.
Delicate and sprawling, this familiar old wall plant has bright yellow, tubular flowers and fern-like foliage. Twisted flower stalks make all the flowers face the same way.

Yellow Horned-poppy *Glaucium flavum* (P)
Height: 1–3ft/30–90cm.
Season: Summer, autumn.
Environment: Sunny border; wall.
Large, floppy, bright yellow flowers are a distinctive sight among the fleshy, greyish-green leaves. It produces curved, slender seed pods which are poisonous.

Yellow Rattle *Rhinanthus minor* (A)
Height: 1–1½/10–40cm.
Season: Summer.

Environment: Sunny border; meadow.
A variable plant with four angled stems, attractive to insects. Self-sowing, it grows well in most soils and has yellow flowers.

Yellow Water-Lily ('Brandy Bottle')
Nuphar lutea (P)
Height: 6in/15cm (above water)
Season: Summer.
Environment: Marsh and Pond.
Dark green, leathery leaves and simple yellow flowers are followed by bottle-shaped fruits.

Fig 135 Yarrow (Achillea millefolium) *makes large, flat-headed white flower clusters against a deep green foliage.*

Appendices

PROTECTED PLANTS IN THE UK

These are currently protected under the terms of the Wildlife and Countryside Act 1981 in the United Kingdom. This forbids any part of the plant to be uprooted or picked; nor seed to be collected. New species are added all the time, so do check in *The British Red Data Book I: Vascular Plants*, from the Royal Society for Nature Conservation. You may be fined up to £500 per plant. It is an offence to uproot any wild plant.

Schedule of Protected Plants

Common name	Scientific name
Adder's-tongue spearwort	*Ranunculus ophioglossifolius*
Alpine catchfly	*Lychnis alpina*
Alpine gentian	*Gentiana nivalis*
Alpine sow-thistle	*Cicerbita alpina*
Alpine woodsia	*Woodsia alpina*
Bedstraw broomrape	*Orobanche caryophyllacea*
Blue heath	*Phyllodoce caerulea*
Brown galingale	*Cyperus fuscus*
Cheddar pink	*Dianthus gratianopolitanus*
Childling pink	*Petrorhagia nanteuilii*
Diapensia	*Diapensia lapponica*
Dickie's bladder-fern	*Cystopteris dickieana*
Downy woundwort	*Stachys germanica*
Drooping saxifrage	*Saxifraga cernua*
Early spider-orchid	*Ophrys sphegodes*
Fen orchid	*Liparis loeselii*
Fen violet	*Viola persicifolia*
Field cow-wheat	*Melampyrum arvense*
Field eryngo	*Eryngium campestre*
Field wormwood	*Artemisia campestris*
Ghost orchid	*Epipogium aphyllum*
Greater-yellow-rattle	*Rhinanthus serotinus*
Jersey cudweed	*Gnaphalium luteoalbum*
Killarney fern	*Trichomanes speciosum*
Lady's slipper	*Cypripedium calceolus*
Late spider-orchid	*Ophrys fuciflora*
Least-lettuce	*Lactuca saligna*
Limestone woundwort	*Stachys alpina*
Lizard orchid	*Himantoglossum hircinum*
Military orchid	*Orchis militaris*
Monkey orchid	*Orchis simia*
Norwegian sandwort	*Arenaria norvegica*
Oblong woodsia	*Woodsia ilvensis*
Oxtongue broomrape	*Orobanche loricata*
Perennial knawel	*Scleranthus perennis*
Plymouth pear	*Pyrus cordata*
Purple spurge	*Euphorbia peplis*
Red helleborine	*Cephalanthera rubra*
Ribbon-leaved water-plantain	*Alisma gramineum*
Rock cinquefoil	*Potentilla rupestris*
Rock sea-lavender (two rare species)	*Limonium paradoxum* / *Limonium recurvum*
Rough marsh-mallow	*Althaea hirsuta*
Round-headed leek	*Allium sphaerocephalon*
Sea knotgrass	*Polygonum maritimum*
Sickle-leaved hare's-ear	*Bupleurum falcatum*
Small Alison	*Alyssum alyssoides*
Small hare's-ear	*Bupleurum baldense*
Snowdon lily	*Lloydia serotina*
Spiked speedwell	*Veronica spicata*
Spring gentian	*Gentiana verna*
Starfruit	*Damasonium alisma*
Starved wood-sedge	*Carex depauperata*
Teesdale sandwort	*Minuartia stricta*
Thistle broomrape	*Orobanche reticulata*
Triangular club-rush	*Scirpus triquetrus*
Tufted saxifrage	*Saxifraga cespitosa*
Water germander	*Teucrium scordium*
Whorled solomon's-seal	*Polygonatum verticillatum*
Wild cotoneaster	*Cotoneaster integerrimus*
Wild gladiolus	*Gladiolus illyricus*
Wood calamint	*Calamintha sylvatica*

GLOSSARY

Acid The term used to describe soil or compost with a pH lower than 7.0.

Alkaline The term used to describe soil or compost with pH higher than 7.0, usually indicating a high lime content.

Alpine A plant that in its natural habitat prefers the thin, rocky soil of mountain terrain and is therefore suited to rock gardens.

Annual Any plant that germinates, grows, blooms, sets seed and dies within a single year.

Bedding Plant An annual plant that is used to provide a seasonal display in beds or containers.

Biennial Any plant that germinates, grows, blooms, sets seed and dies within a two-year period.

Bog An area of waterlogged land, usually very acidic, suited to plants that like to grow with their roots in permanently moist soil.

Broadcast To sow or scatter seed over the soil instead of in rows.

Bulb A plant storage organ containing food for a 'resting' period and comprising fleshy scales or a swollen leaf base.

Bulbils Small bulbs found clustered at the base of some plants which can be detached and grown into full-sized bulbs.

Calcareous The term applied to soil or compost containing a large percentage of chalk or lime. It is therefore alkaline.

Calcifuge A plant that will not tolerate a high lime content soil.

Chalk The common term applied to the compound calcium carbonate, identical (chemically) to limestone. It is usually applied to acid soil or compost as hydrated lime to increase its pH level.

Clay The term applied to soil or compost comprising a mixture of fine sand and wet, sticky alumina. Difficult to work but fertile if treated.

Compost Either rotted down vegetable material producing a fertile humus or a specially prepared soil mixture.

Conifer A tree bearing cones.

Corm A plant storage organ comprising a thickened underground stem.

Deciduous The term applied to any plant that loses its leaves in winter.

Evergreen The term applied to any plant that loses and replaces its leaves gradually throughout the seasons.

Exotic Any plant not indigenous to the country in which it is growing. Unable to naturalize.

Ground cover Dense, low-growing shrubby plants that closely cover the soil.

Habit The size and manner of growth of a plant, such as 'upright', 'creeping', etc.

Habitat The natural living area or the conditions under which a plant grows.

Half-hardy The term applied to any winter-tender plant that requires protection in the colder months.

Hedgerow A hedge, usually made up of several wild species and sometimes incorporating a bank or ditch.

Herbaceous The term applied to any plant which makes soft, sappy growth rather than the woody growth of a shrub or tree, for example.

Humus Rotted down organic matter used as soil-building fertilizer.

Hybrid A cross between plants of different species, usually designed to refine particular attributes.

Indigenous The term applied to a plant that is native to that area.

Laying The technique of splitting, bending and staking hedgerow saplings to shorten and thicken the hedge.

Limestone Naturally occurring rock producing a surface soil with a high pH (i.e. an alkaline soil). Chemically limestone is identical to chalk since both are calcium carbonate.

Marginal The term applied to those plants which grow in the shallows at the edge of a pool or pond.

Marsh An area of land that is waterlogged at all times.

Moraine A bed of small stones or grit watered from below and particularly suitable for growing alpine plants.

Native The term applied to any plant that naturally occurs in its locality or country.

Naturalize To grow plants under conditions as close as possible to those found in their natural habitat; imported plants can be naturalized by allowing them to self-seed and establish themselves in the wild.

Oxygenating The term applied to any plant which grows in or under water and which gives off significant levels of oxygen.

Perennial Any plant which lives and flowers for a number of years.

Raceme An unbranched flower spike with the flowers carried on equal length stalks.

Rhizome An underground stem, usually growing horizontally, which produces shoots some distance from the parent plant.

Root ball A cluster of plant roots and soil.

Runner A plant shoot that roots at intervals along its length.

Species A group of plants that share the same characteristics and which will interbreed.

Taproot The main, straight root of a plant, thicker at the top than at the base from which subsidiary rootlets grow.

Toxic Poisonous.

Variegated Foliage marked with contrasting coloured spots, stripes or blotches due to some mutation such as a benign virus or mineral deficiency.

Variety Either a group of plants within a species or a plant with particularly distinctive characteristics.

Vernalization The technique by which seeds or bulbs are exposed to low temperatures to imitate a natural winter and encourage either germination or flowers.

Index